Around the World in Eighty Years

An Odyssey on Wings of Discovery

By

Ralph H. Miner

PublishAmerica
Baltimore

First printing

At the specific preference of the author, PublishAmerica allowed this work to remain exactly as the author intended, verbatim, without editorial input.

Cover Design By Marija Miletic Dail

ISBN: 1-4137-8268-X
PUBLISHED BY PUBLISHAMERICA, LLLP
www.publishamerica.com
Baltimore

Printed in the United States of America

Dedicated To My Wife Rosemary

Contents

Introduction

Dear Reader:

Some eighty years ago, sitting on my father's lap in the open cockpit of an ancient biplane, my dad had engaged a barnstorming pilot to take us up on our first airplane ride. We took off from my grandfather's farm on an exciting and glorious experience. Though a small child at the time, a passion for flying was born which proved to be far more deeply imbedded than mere childhood fantasy. I could not know, of course, the extremes to which this passion for flying would one day carry me.

The odyssey on wings of discovery has been structured along autobiographical lines. This format enables sharing with the reader how the fates conspired to carry one individual into not only unexpectedly intense flying adventures, but into career paths which yielded some unique insights into the conduct of science and technology at large. However, attempts to apply those insights, often challenging the conventional wisdom, while occasionally making limited gains, also involved some mistakes and professional setbacks.

All of the above not only had a profound effect on my personal and professional life, but left me with the feeling that my experiences—mistakes and all—could be meaningfully shared with generations past, present and future. Yes, viewpoints do change from generation to generation, but those ethical and spiritual core values, which should move all people toward coherent and productive life systems, do not change. Core values only shift in the perspective from which they are viewed as people move from era to era in a climate of continuing explosive world growth.

Hence, offered in this book is a wide-ranging Around The World In Eighty Years. The reader will find adventure, tragedy, pathos, angel intervention, the politics of military and corporate professional behavior... and, finally, an ethically premised advocacy on the conduct of science and technology.

I encouragingly share this odyssey with you, the reader, on wings of discovery and metaphors of flight.

Sincerely,

Ralph H. Miner
Carmel, California

Prologue
Charting the Course

Our take off from Assam Valley, India, was on a cold December night in 1944. Our flight was from India to China over the formidable mountains of Northern Tibet—the infamous Himalayan Hump of World War II. Our aircraft was a four engine B-24 Liberator converted to a cargo carrier. Our mission was to deliver drums of fuel to the B-29 bombers operating out of Western China.

An hour after reaching cruising altitude in a night of filthy weather, we found ourselves flying into the teeth of a particularly violent thunderstorm. Now, this is not speaking of a flight in a modern jet transport soaring easily above forty thousand feet with an overabundance of thrust horsepower and storm avoidance radar. I'm speaking of an underpowered, overloaded, four engine transport aircraft with no storm avoidance radar, no wing deicer system and the most primitive instrument flying and navigational aids. Our converted B-24 was never intended for the operational tasks it was required to assume in the kind of weather and high altitude flying encountered across Northern Tibet.

At a period in flight history when jet stream wind phenomena was virtually unheard of, we experienced the weirdest weather imaginable as jet stream winds of up to two-hundred mph slammed against twenty-thousand foot mountains, forging upward thrusting wind convection currents to unbelievable powerful updrafts and towering thunderheads. Here, indeed, was the mother of all weather systems!…Sadly, we lost far too many of our aircraft and flight crews to these treacherous conditions.

But there was no pulling off the shoulder of the road to wait out the storm. One's encapsulation in those three dimensions of space and one dimension of time was there to reckoned with... Now! ... Without pause!

Myriad aspects of the flight associated with reaching our destination in China must be handled with unrelenting presence of mind. Firstly, the nature of fear must be understood and then held in detached abeyance during exposure to persistent extreme turbulence of unknown dimensions, while surrounded by blinding lightning flashes and being tossed about the sky like a cork.

Parenthetically, both the nature and intensity of fear involved in life-threatening flight situations will be shared, as well as the approach to the handling of these fears; and, perhaps strangely to some, an incomparable kind of joy in keeping fear in abeyance in overcoming dangerous situations.

Intense diligence had to be maintained in dealing with the present situation entirely by reference to flight instruments, while at the same time bearing in mind the proximity of inordinately high mountain peaks—rock piles not at all sympathetic to the up and down altitude changes imposed by the whims of turbulence. Then, too, as an ungainly load of wing ice began to accumulate—our aircraft had no wing deicer system—power had to be sharply increased while taking care not to overcompensate for sluggish flight control response. Still, the control wheel had to be smartly wrenched left and right from time to time in order to break the ice free of the wing's aileron control hinges. Then, added to it all, were machine gun sounds as ice breaking off the propellers was flung against the fuselage just behind the cockpit; with a further invitation to distraction caused by fingers of static electricity dancing around the windshield along with impacting sleet. Combined with the blinding lightning flashes and extreme turbulence, it was very difficult to avoid becoming detached from one's only available sensory extension—the instrument flight panel. Our flying was all hands-on. We had no auto pilot systems.

Now, as if all that were not enough, we had to bear in mind navigation and time-to-destination factors as well as the imminent possibility of having to dump cargo weight in order to handle our load of wing ice without a prohibitive drop in altitude. We were now operating at full power, which normally is permitted for only short periods. This is in order not to exceed prohibitive engine temperature limits. We were trying to squeak over the last mountain ridge and into our normal descent into China. This time we made it without dumping our cargo, though pushing deeply into the red warning zone of the upper limits of engine temperature. The moment we crossed the last mountain ridge, power was sharply reduced as we started our descent, shedding wing ice all the way down.

Weaving all of the parts of operational flight into one whole system fabric while apportioning a relentless, unforgiving time and space budget into one seamless system was the name of the game. Indeed, the requirement for unrelenting presence of mind while simultaneously juggling many life or death factors, stood unabated until a primitively facilitated instrument approach to the airfield in Chengtu, China was made and the wheels of the landing gear crunched the runway. With a great sigh of relief, a diligently addressed operational mission was brought to a successful end. Sadly, this was not always the case; but this time around, the "fabric" of the operational system had been strained, but not torn.

In all of this, too, is the vital importance of the pilot's sense of "scanning." Scanning is too often undervalued by some pilots. Scanning is the disciplined practice of constantly sweeping the whole of the operational flight situation in *all* of its aspects—not allowing inordinate focus on any single aspect of the flight at the expense of falling short on the whole of things. I shall enlarge on the scanning aspect in other chapters, since it is a discipline which can carry over into all aspects of life. It is a practice which can improve life as well as intercept misjudgments in one's approach to various life situations. However, I'm the first to admit that while my scanning performance in the cockpit rates rather well, I did not always practice scanning as I should have in the ground based environment.

So, while the time-constrained, three-dimensional world of flight holds life or death issues in an immediate time frame, the two-dimensional life is viewed from a different, perhaps too casual perspective.

In the two-dimensional world, one's life is lived in a myriad of fragmented systems and unfulfilled responses to the urgency of dealing with certain life-endangering system deficiencies. Even in the light of the fixed, inflexible relentlessness of clock and calendar time, we are not reckoning in a timely manner with the pile up of those events which can have a deteriorating effect not only on our personal lives, but on our total ecology as well.

Unlike the relentless life or death demands of three-dimensional flight, the life or death ultimate consequences of a diminished ecology are not readily seen from the two-dimensional earthbound viewpoint. With our feet firmly planted on the ground, no immediate time decisions seem necessary. We sit on a park bench and admire the view. We have a beer. We seem to be surviving. But we are harboring only an illusion of survival!

For quite some time, people at large, in an abstract, whimsical way, have casually viewed themselves as passengers on the Space Ship Earth. But the time for setting aside the abstract, whimsical view is long overdue. It is suggested that there is a very strong parallel between the micro-level of individual flight by man and the macro-level of Planet Earth's flight through time and space. Earthlings, too, are "in flight." The flight of the planet is now fraught with imminent danger to the survival of its passengers who, like the individual aircraft pilot, are in reality all encapsulated in three dimensions of space and one dimension of time. Survival, then, is a matter of responding to a new appreciation of the relentless dictates of time and the demands of the critically diminished ecological systems of the planet.

At this dawn of the new century, we find ourselves conducting our lives in a world of explosive, virtually uncontrolled, fragmented systems growth and radical change—all compressed within a heretofore unprecedented short period of time. All of this is simply uncontainable on the long term unless we develop an enhanced appreciation by world society of their collective responsibility—their responsibility to better understand their role in pressing for political and industrial response to the survival of our planet. While present limited actions toward that end are to be appreciated, these are relatively feeble actions and are woefully out of sync—*time wise*—with immediate as well as future ecosystem needs.

In summary of the prologue, an oversimplification of the basic thesis of this book is that those who live in the two-dimensional world could benefit from a better understanding of the systems and disciplines of the three-dimensional comprehensiveness found in metaphors of flight. Of all the activities one might engage in, the act of flying, free of the earth, operating in three dimensions of space and one dimension of time, holds a totality of operational system, an imposition of relentless time constraints on fulfilling the demands of that system, and a finality of decision-making pressures unlike most other human activities.

To the ends of encouraging an enhanced appreciation of the deeper meaning of flight, and noting a strong general interest in the romance of flight, the writer feels that perhaps the broader aspects of the discovery process and the often unique behavior of operational systems, usefully paralleled in metaphors of flight, could be widely shared.

Observing people's general interests, it is noted that whether young or old, whether pilot or nonpilot, there is not only a strong on-going interest in the romance of flight, but there seems to be a still growing interest in antique airplanes and the war birds of World War II.

This book seeks to interact with that interest and to share the discoveries of one man through the adventures and inspirations of flight. I have had the privilege of piloting all types of fighters, bombers and transport aircraft all over the world from the arctic circle of Greenland and Iceland, to Europe, to the equatorial regions of Africa and South America, and to India, Tibet, Burma, China, the South Pacific and Greater Asia. In many thousands of hours of flying, my consciousness was moved toward an increasing awe of the grandeur and beautiful texture of our planet as well as the varieties of people and life styles inhabiting the thin skin of earth's biosphere... I continue to believe there exists the wholeness of some yet to be understood Divine Plan for our collective existence.

Yet, why has such grandeur become so severely tarnished in the time span of a mere century?...A large part of the answer, I believe, lies in an over-compartmentalized structure of society's belief systems. The truly holistic systems viewpoint has not yet permeated the minds of those leaders who have loosely woven the threads of science, technology and politics into an ungainly, patched together set of world systems. Indeed, the truly holistic viewpoint is still overwhelmingly outvoted.

Hence, intermeshed with flying experiences, observations will be offered on the conduct of professional life—mine and others—in often intense military, political and technological environments... with, of course, a useful accounting of regrets and mistakes along the way—experiences and mistakes which the reader might wish to consider as he weighs the conduct of his own personal and professional life.

It must also be noted that this book can be approached two ways: one, it can be found simply as a rather interesting collection of flying adventures... or, two, it can offer the reader fresh perspective, enhancing both his personal and professional outlook and perhaps stimulating his sense of social responsibility toward the urgency of safeguarding our collective destiny.

Quoting Astronaut-Scientist, Dr. Edgar Mitchell, he said: "The crew of Space Ship Earth is in virtual mutiny to the order of the universe."

In any case, we are all entitled to grow in holistic wisdom and to claim our spiritual heritage and its promise of the good life while working our way through the secular world. Though many of us find ourselves stumbling at times, God has infinite patience. Do become airborne, at least in the spirit of metaphor, on your own wings of discovery.

Chapter One
Flying Toward an Enlarged Perspective
Absorbing Incredible Global Diversity

"This is Air Force Four-Three-Seven calling Greenland Outer Island Control...Over."

"Air Force Four-Three-Seven, this is Island Control...Go ahead."

"Air Force Four-Three-Seven, twenty miles west of Greenland on instruments at seven-thousand feet. Requesting approach and landing instructions...Over."

"Air Force Four-Three-Seven, you are cleared to descend to one-thousand feet at Island Control. Present ceiling two thousand feet. Altimeter setting two-nine-point-eight-seven. Visibility six miles. Wind west at ten. You are cleared to the Blewie West landing strip via the Igalaco Fjord. Make sure you pass Island Control under the overcast. As you approach the mouth of the fjord, descend to five hundred feet and reduce speed. Be advised that cloud cover is over the cliffs to each side of the fjord. You are flying into a no-turn-around tunnel...Watch it, friend!... And welcome to Greenland!"

"Four-Three-Seven. Acknowledged... And thanks, Control." Entering the mouth of the Igalaco Fjord, speed was reduced to just under two hundred in order to keep events in "the tunnel" from happening too fast. As it was, the weather in the fjord had worsened since getting my clearance from Outer Island Control. I soon found myself tickling the tops of the protruding icebergs as turns in the fjord were navigated, while paying close attention to the walls of the cliffs to either side. Indeed, it was far too busy a time to take in the spectacular beauty of it all. Moreover, drifting mists were further obscuring visibility. I *must not* allow myself to get into an instrument flight condition. Avoidance of the cliffs on an instrument climb-out would have been next to impossible.

Further complicating visibility was a poorly designed flat cockpit canopy that restricted not only forward visibility, but visibility downward between protruding engine nacelles and the fuselage. A bubble-type canopy was desperately needed on this aircraft. (Upon my return from England, I urged the aircraft's design people to initiate such a design change since the operational combat pilots also objected to this same situation… A bubble canopy was soon on the production line.)

Parenthetically, I should also mention that my first stop out of the U.S. before starting across the North Atlantic was Goose Bay, Labrador. Stuck there for a few days on weather delays, I studied intensely the large relief map of Greenland in the flight operations office. It offered a choice of one of three fjords from Outer Island Control, depending on weather, as waterway routes to the inland landing strip at Blewie West. The relief map revealed dead end canyons, the most tempting one warned of by a clearly visible, partially sunken ship, together with other distinguishing features and rock outcroppings. Clearly, that relief map was a vital contribution to a successful first time flight into Greenland…

Oh! There's my landing readiness signal—a uniquely protruding rock outcropping. No landing strip in sight yet as speed was reduced to one-thirty. Landing gear was extended and full wing flaps applied while anticipating the next sharp turn in the fjord. There it was! An uphill steel landing mat laid out on the glacier at the end of the fjord… A big sigh of relief as the wheels crunched the mat. Whew! That flight was a real adrenaline booster. But the first leg of my 1944 North Atlantic flight was complete.

A weather layover was necessary since the reverse-direction down hill take off and circle to climb out over the glacier to the top of the mountains could be safely executed only in good weather… Two days later, weather clear enough.

The often ominous stretch of the North Atlantic Sea between

Greenland and Iceland was very choppy that morning. The hungry growl of two powerful engines told of chewing up the air with a certain fury as I flew in and out of turbulent storm squalls a few thousand feet above the iceberg-strewn surface of the sea.

My assignment was to fly to England during World War II to deliver one of the first of a powerful new attack bomber, the A-26, hardly out of the test and development stage. Indeed, with no provision for a copilot, no automatic pilot and no oxygen system, not to mention a number of development bugs still being worked out, this beautiful new airplane offered more than its fair share of flight gremlins—strange noises and transient vibrational modes— psychologically amplified by the ominous flight environment. Gremlins usually have a way of hiding themselves when one is flying over flat land in calm, clear sunlight. But given unusual circumstances, the gremlins come out to dance—particularly when one is flying an admittedly still-in-development new aircraft.

Whoa!... That was no gremlin! That one called for a real wrench to the gut!... After uneventfully crossing half of the North Atlantic Ocean, the right engine began unceremoniously cutting out... intermittently. Apparently an earlier fuel feed problem had not been fully resolved. I recalled an occasion involving this new model wherein an unfortunate pilot experienced simultaneous fuel feed failure on both engines shortly after take off, but safely belly landed in an empty field. Possible double engine failure did cross my mind along with the extremely unattractive prospect of ditching in the North Atlantic Sea. Even if the icebergs were safely circumvented, the prospect of making a quick exit from a cockpit whose sluggish canopy locking devices were of faulty design, let alone the obviously frigid water temperature, posed considerable alarm.

Yes, the situation was very frightening and found me quite apprehensive. What the hell was a young kid like me doing in this situation anyway?...

I had left a cozy war-draft-exempt job as a junior design engineer with a major aircraft firm, a company producing military aircraft. In the coffee-sipping environment of the design room, the most serious danger, of course, was the possibility of leaving a coffee cup stain on one's drawing. It was necessary to do some heavy persuading in order to get a release from my draft exempt position. But as an already licensed commercial pilot, a direct commission as an Air Force flight officer with the Air Transport Command awaited. This offered the promise of immediate operational flying in all types of fighters, bombers and transport aircraft to destinations all over the world. I had always felt that a properly rounded aeronautical engineer should embrace the broadest possible experience as an operational pilot, adding balance to an overwhelming population of competent but non-flying aeronautical engineers.

So, with the support of my understanding wife, I left the cozy environs of the company's engineering department and reported to the Air Transport Command's base in Long Beach, California. Flying had been a passion with me from teen years, a passion deeply enjoyed... most of the time. This particular morning was not one of those times!

Halfway between Greenland and Reykjavic, Iceland it was decided to make a fresh calculation of my estimated time of arrival in Iceland—reaching for my pocket computer, a thin circular slide rule for computing time and distance, true airspeed, etc. The computer was in the large left pocket of my freshly laundered shirt put on in Greenland just that morning. My dear wife, who packed my travel bag, had a loving habit of putting little notes in my fresh shirt pockets. Having dressed hurriedly that morning, my computer was shoved in the pocket without discovering her latest note. This particular morning, the note had become wedged in between the plastic dials of the computer. That note, discovered during this in-flight emergency, so focused my sense of prayer that it was carried in my wallet until it literally fell apart. The note read: *Dearest husband: Always remember this passage from the Bible... "If I take the wings of the morning and dwell in the uttermost parts of the sea, even there shall thy hand lead me, and thy right hand shall hold me."*

Clearly, there could be no more "uttermost part of the sea" than my present flight path. But the gut wrenching fear left immediately, leaving me with useful apprehension. Experimenting with reduced power settings and fuel mixture variations, the left engine held true and while the right engine continued its intermittent cutting out, the Iceland landfall finally welcomed me and the landing in Reykjavic was uneventful.

A few days later, following discussion with the aircraft company, the correction was made. Annoying enough, correction had already been made on the production line, but the company had failed to send me the customary Defect Correction Bulletin. But no harm done... this time...

So, on to England, finding out later that many of our aircraft were held up in Iceland for almost a week until after D-Day. We were also warned by the operations officer to be on our toes with our compass navigation and not be lured into a false radio beam into Germany. We then took off for the Air Base in Prestwick, Scotland, our first stop in the British Isles.

The trip was completed without enemy interference. I had to fire the friend-or-foe, color-of-the-day flare only once when a couple of British fighters pulled along side. The distinctly different silhouette of this beautiful new bomber was a stranger to British wartime skies.

After a pleasant few days introducing the new bomber to the operational group, and after their friendly response to my desire to fly the British Spitfire Fighter, it was time to determine how to make my return to the United States. No advance planning had been made for this.

The Operations Officer asked what my Air Force pilot rating was. Happily, he was advised that mine was a "Five P" pilot rating, which certified qualifications as aircraft commander on any type of fighter, bomber or transport aircraft operated by the U.S. Air Force.

"Good," he said, "then we have some options. For one thing, we are returning a war weary B-17 to the Aberdeen Proving Ground north of Washington, D.C. via Africa and South America. First stop out of England would be Casablanca. Are you interested?"

"Yes, indeed! I have a brother stationed at the Naval Base in Port

Lyautey, north of Casablanca."

"Fine," he said, "we have a crew for you of men due to return to the States. Lt. Jim Calvin will be your copilot, Lt. Carl Sorenson your navigator and Sgt. Ted Keys, your flight engineer."

"Great! Where do we meet and when do we leave?"

"You meet them in London tomorrow, packed and ready."

"That's O.K. It's more than O.K. This means I'll have time to call on the good friend I grew up with in my home neighborhood." Johnny Werner was a waist gunner in one of the B-17 bomb groups. Fortunately, he had jus returned from a mission and was available on my short time schedule. After a few hours joyful visit, promising to call on his mom and dad upon my return, I was off to London. That later call was a sad one since they had been advised he had been shot down over Germany shortly after my visit with him. He had successfully bailed out, however, and spent the rest of the war in a German prison camp... Obviously, a happy reunion after the war.

After a sleepless night in London, listening for the random cutoffs of German buzz bomb engines, wondering where in London they would fall, while at the same time praying for myself and the people of that great city, we moved on down to the air base on the southern tip of England. A few days of patching flak holes and tuning four tired engines on this war weary old beauty and we were ready to fly.

Just after dark, a few seconds worth of butterflies in the gut, and we opened the throttles on our fully loaded old B-17 and took off for an all night flight to Casablanca. The first leg of our flight was out to sea, far off the coast of France and Portugal, to our assigned earth meridian. Then due south on that meridian until abreast of Gibralter, and from that point the final leg of the flight to North Africa. Our last view of human life that night was a large flotilla of ships moving without lights under a misty quarter moon.

As the quarter moon disappeared, we found ourselves flying in a very still, crystal clear night with the brightest possible canopy of stars. Not all pilots share this, but I've always found flying at night for protracted periods over open sea, with no other sign of human life, one of the loneliest ways to fly... that is, from the perspective of the aircraft commander who has the ultimate responsibility for dealing with and integrating myriad variables and contingencies incident to reaching the planned destination. But then, on the other hand, free of bad weather on this stillest of nights, with the brightest stars on the horizon reflecting jewels on the crests of the ocean swells, an invitation to contemplative thought presented itself.

With a half-gallon jug of black coffee at my side, not fully trusting the mechanical integrity of this old bird, I planned an all night vigil, personally monitoring the behavior of its various systems. But for the present, at least, with the crew dozing and all four engines comfortably settled into the harmonious drone of the cruise mode, I turned my eyes to the stars to do what many people do under inspiring circumstances—yield one's self to a what's-it-all-about mood.

One at once feels himself a speck in the immensity of all things...which he is. Indeed, much less than a speck in a physical sense. But let his mind wander deep into the abyss of space, exposing himself to his soul sense, and the spirituality of it all invites him to be more directly cognizant of his Creator... and, suddenly, he isn't lonely anymore. He becomes one with a sense of the Eternity of Life. At that point, an unspeakable sense of peace and joy embraced me. This peace and joy while in flight had been experienced many times in various situations, but needed was the self-assurance granted by this particularly poignant experience.

It would seem that the sweeping operational demands of World War II had thrust tasks upon young pilots, which, in normal times, would have been found unthinkable without the backup of many, many years of flying experience. Even the normal training procedure of an instructor pilot checking the young flight commander on his first flight to any new foreign destination was set aside. Wartime urgencies simply precluded traditional flight experience requirements and training procedures. In short, it was a kind of on-the-job training by one's self.

One often thinks of a poem written in 1941 by wartime pilot, John Magee, which beautifully expresses the deepest feelings of anyone who loves to fly. With deep appreciation that poem is quoted here:

"Oh, I have slipped the surly bonds of earth
And danced the skies on laughter silvered wings;
Sunward I've climbed and joined the tumbling mirth
Of sun split clouds—and done a hundred things
You have not dreamed of—Wheeled and soared and swung
High in the sunlit silence. Hov'ring there
I've chased the shouting wind along,
And flung my eager craft through footless halls of air.
Up, up the long, delirious, burning blue
I've topped the wind-swept heights with easy grace
Where never lark, or even eagle flew.
And, while with silent, lifting mind I've trod
The high untrespassed sanctity of space,
Put out my hand, and touched the face of God."

That poem became quite famous and stands high even today in the flying community, often likened to the poetic prose of pioneer pilot Antoine de St. Exupery in his classic book, "Wind Sand and Stars"—required reading for pilots young and old or for anyone interested in the romance of flight.

Our flight at this point in time, based on estimated distance flown on our present compass heading, says we should be abreast of Gibralter on our assigned meridian within thirty minutes. Time to alert Carl to confirm our position with a star fix and we'll make our left turn for North Africa.

Halfway inbound on the last leg of our flight, the horizon presented the edge of a golden dawn. The growing light of day, however, also revealed something else. A severe oil leak was flowing from the now clearly visible number three engine cowling. Yet, the oil reservoir was not exhausted in that the oil pressure on that engine remained constant. Upon discussion with Jim and Ted, we agreed that since we were getting low on fuel, we would remain in the four engine cruise mode and not shut down number three until the oil pressure fluctuated. Since we were experiencing greater fuel consumption than expected, operating at increased power on three engines would, of course, sharply increase fuel consumption.

Hey, now! A smug smile on my face. Here was my excuse to land at the nearest African landfall—the Naval Air Base where my brother was stationed. It's not that the Navy objects to hosting an Air Force aircraft, but my Air Force boss would prefer that we land at our assigned destination. Since how to arrange a meeting with my brother hadn't yet been worked out and only knowing that one way or another we were going to meet—not having seen him for two years—this mild emergency was a very neat way of doing it.

So, after an instrument approach through a low cloud cover under good conditions, we were on the friendly ground once again. After reporting our arrival in Port Lyautey to Casablanca Operations and arranging for a Navy mechanic to assist my flight engineer in his work on number three engine, it was determined that my brother had returned from patrol duty and was on the base. I had the great pleasure of rousting him out of his bed, much to his blinking surprise.

After a happy day's visit and a few nuts and hose clamps tightened on Number Three, we took off and reported to our Casablanca base down the Moroccan coast.

The next day, however, while flying on top of the dust storms across the Sahara Desert, old Number Three just plain laid down and died. After feathering the propeller and shutting down the engine, we landed an hour later at Dakar in Senegal's good weather, but quite low on fuel. This old bird was a bit of a gas hog. A few days in Dakar and the engine was replaced.

We took off down the African coast for Liberia and within an hour found ourselves in solid instrument flying conditions and literally saw nothing until we broke out of the soup on an instrument approach to the jungle landing strip in Liberia—a shocking intense green in contrast to Sahara.

This was, indeed, becoming a trip of wide environmental and ecosystem contrasts. Sleeping in a grass hut up on stilts in a driving rainstorm with a cluster of chanting natives huddled under the floor invited a whole set of new thought patterns. Thoughts ranged over a mere few days from the icebergs of the Arctic Circle to the aridness of the Sahara Desert to the humid jungle of Equatorial Africa. Many years later, feelings about these contrasts would surface in my studies of the global ecosystem and its economic patterns.

The next day we took off for Ascension Island, a tiny dot of land just below the equator in the middle of the South Atlantic Ocean—hardly large enough to contain the air base.

From Ascension Island we flew to Natal on the coast of South America. Following another careful mechanical inspection of our airplane, we were off to Belem, still in that vast country of Brazil.

The day after that, we had a relatively short run to Georgetown in the small country of Guyana, with plenty of reserve fuel to satisfy some of my curiosity about that great Amazon River. We took a short, very low altitude, thirty-mile trip up the Amazon, noting with interest the virtually untouched density of the beautiful rain forest.

A few decades later, I could only register shock over a magazine article showing the incredible ravages of the rain forest of the Amazon in all too short a period of time.

Over the next three days, after cautious stops in Puerto Rico and Miami for inspection of the safety aspects of oil leaks, a continuing survey of possible reasons for inordinate fuel consumption, and automatic propeller pitch control that would no longer hold its cruise setting, and sluggish landing gear and wing flap actuation systems, we took off for the last leg of our journey. We landed at Aberdeen Proving Ground north of Washington shortly after midnight in good weather... and with profound thanks to this proud old B-17 which, in spite of its numerous mechanical ailments, saw us safely home.

The next day, after bidding goodbye to Jim, Carl and Ted—a fine crew who were remaining on the east coast—the Aberdeen Operations Officer greeted me with good news. He had a P-51 to be returned to the factory in California.

Notwithstanding the enjoyable companionship of my B-17 crew, it was always a good feeling to be flying solo again in a swift airplane. For me, invitations to introspective thought were more poignantly felt when flying solo in the higher reaches of the sky. Moreover, in hardly any time at all, home at last with my lovely wife in Long Beach, California.

In summary of this journey, it must be said that it offered a highly diversified perspective of the world's many sociological and ecological structures. This very wide flight loop across America, the North Atlantic Ocean via Labrador, Greenland, Iceland, to war-torn England; then on past France and Portugal to North Africa, across the Sahara Desert to Equatorial Africa, across the South Atlantic to Brazil and on up to the Amazon River Area, on to Puerto Rico, Miami and Washington, D.C. and then finally back to the Pacific Coast— notwithstanding bouts with severe weather, falling bombs and a few touchy in-flight mechanical problems with my airplanes—all went rather smoothly, since I had not previously flown any of these routes.

I must also make note of American and British military efficiency. No matter how remote, primitively facilitated, near-impossible logistics or subject to falling bombs, the ground-based operational support systems functioned remarkably well.

It must be underscored that a fine *espirit de corps* existed in the ground-based support people's appreciation that those of us engaged in flight operations were locked into an inescapable commitment to three dimensions of space and one dimension of time. We simply could not function without reliable support from the ground people. Their servicing of our flying machines, their operation and maintenance of crucial radio communication and navigation systems, their readiness in dealing with crash situations, etc., etc. were most commendable.

Notwithstanding my maverick-like reaction to occasional procedural glitches here and there, I could only observe that military operational planning and management techniques are of such high order value that they ought to be infused into an anemic civilian education system. That is, the education system at large has always been weak in teaching interdisciplinary thinking and the planning and management of vast interlocking systems.

I should underscore, however, that notwithstanding my strong endorsement of the military's operational system planning and management techniques, I am not, by nature, a military person. I was simply a maverick civilian in military uniform. My maverickness emerges in later chapters.

So, after all too brief a holiday with my wife, I reported back to my Air Transport command base where, as head of the Medium Bomber Flight Transition School, I was ready to resume my flight instructor duties and stay home for a while.

However, a real surprise awaited. Half of the base's pilots, including myself, were being transferred to the infamous Northern India-China Himalayan Hump flying operation.

While not wanting to leave the country again quite so soon, I was at least grateful that this most difficult wartime assignment did not occur during my lower level of flying experience. At this time of final Air Force assignment, I was as ready as I was ever going to be, though admittedly with some trepidation... The immediate future awaited.

Chapter Two
The Early Years
Uncertainty, Awakening, Going For It

In this chapter, the flow of an eighty year odyssey is interrupted to share the importance of coming to grips with uncertainties as to one's potential abilities and aptitudes and awakening to one's ultimate role in life's processes. I'm sure there are many people out there who are not recognizing their true potential. In my own case, while I suppose my childhood and growing up years were in most respects normal enough, I endured an unusually wide gap in transitioning from uncertainty and a lack of self confidence to an eventual awakening and, finally, "going for it." Also included is a sharing of some of the special problems one encounters if he has the questionable good fortune to be born a maverick... Hence, this chapter.

In my own case, I must begin with my very good fortune in having loving parents who had difficulty dealing with me at times, but did not give up. They were of modest means, yet my civil-service-employee father was a good manager of family resources and saw his wife and two sons comfortably through the great depression years.

Both parents were avid outdoor people. Born of mid-western farm families, raised in the sod-constructed farm houses of the late 1800's, each of them migrated west, meeting in 1915 in that large village known as Los Angeles. After marriage, they settled in the house I was to be born in and became suburbanites. However, as outdoor loving people, many weekend camping and vacation trips became the order of things.

In the days long before freeways and consistently good roads, my first trip was when my dad packed up the family, including my baby brother, and took off in our brand new 1923 Dodge touring car for my grandparents' farm in the small farm town of Dunning, Nebraska.

This was a beautiful trip that I was barely old enough to appreciate. After each day of travel, we camped by streams in mountain forests, or by some lake, or anywhere on the Great Plains we happened to be at nightfall. Finally, we arrived late one night at my grandparents' farmhouse.

Some of my earliest childhood memories are of this trip, not the least of which was my first airplane ride by a barnstorming pilot flying off grandfather's farm. Sitting on my dad's lap in the open cockpit of an ancient biplane, this flight was beyond childhood fantasy, since it launched the birth of a lasting passion for flying.

Another nostalgic memory, though a simple one, was riding along side my grandfather in his horse drawn wagon along the Dismal River, which bordered his celery farm. Wafted on a gentle breeze, the exquisite aroma of the blend of river smells and the celery fields for some reason never left me. At once, a simple yet profound childhood memory.

Early childhood was largely a blissful study of cloud forms, petting my dog and playing with toy airplanes. Then came the early school years. While reading, writing and arithmetic were reluctantly acknowledged as must do, I absolutely loathed school in general all the way up to my stumbling through high school with average grades. I'm not proud of this and I mention it for the purpose of sharing an eventual awakening.

I had little self-confidence, did not go out for sports and did not participate in school social activities—I was so shy that I dated very few girls—and was generally credited by my teachers as not a promising student. Among other things, I simply didn't give a damn on what date Eli Whitney invented the cotton gin; not to mention a myriad of other meaningless dates we were required to memorize. I can still see the long pointing finger of my history teacher, humiliating me in front of the whole class as he virtually shouted at me: "Boy, I promise you will be one of life's failures, staring out the window the way you do." For me, school in general never bothered to drive home the idea, quite apart from its lack of relevancy, that what was being taught would at least bear somewhat on my ability to think and eventually aid in picking a role in life. For not only was I a loner, but there were early unrecognized signs of maverickness in my psyche.

Parenthetically, a maverick is a person who takes an independent stand—a person who with good reason, hopefully, refuses at times to conform to the dictates of the conventional wisdom. I will share in greater depth, throughout the book, the pluses and minuses of being stamped a maverick. Much professional pain can arise if one does not handle himself with restraint—which I often did not. On large issues, there is often the danger to one's career of being ethically correct and politically incorrect. I'm sure there are many people out there who need to reckon with maverickness in their make up. If one is famous, being a maverick is more than likely to be viewed with applause. On the other hand, if one is part of that vast community of nonfamous people, like myself, maverickness is often very difficult to deal with… Much more later, not only on the uncertainties, but on the hidden productive potential in living on the path of the maverick.

But for now, back to the earliest years. For all of my loathing of public school, there was the plus side of life as well. Though my parents were unable to persuade me to join the Boy Scouts of America, I did participate intensely in our informal hiking, camping and fishing club. Comprised of four neighborhood boys, we hiked and fished extensively off the trails of the High Sierras on down to the mountains of Southern California.

At the early age of nine, I was building and flying model airplanes, and selling newspapers for pocket money and model airplane supplies. At fourteen, I was sweeping out hangars and wiping down airplanes in exchange for flying lessons, while augmenting my pocket money with a newspaper route. Though still an indifferent public school student, my uncertainty was temporarily set aside in the cockpit and on the mountain trail. But self-confidence continued to wither in the public school environment and in any encounter with officialdom.

Enter, again, my parents. Although they couldn't reach me on the importance of good school performance, they did, however, insist on my building a solid protestant footing through early Bible study and eventual church membership. I at least absorbed an early love of God, along with a fairly reasonable teenage behavior.

In any case, that inevitable day of reckoning finally arrived— graduation from high school, with only average grades, and all. What now? I'm ashamed to admit that I had given no serious thought as to how to make a living. I was beginning to realize that I couldn't survive too well on a newspaper route or as an airport bum sweeping out airplane hangars.

At this point, my flying instructor and friend, Steve Carlson, who seemed to see more in me than I saw in myself, said: "Here's a couple of free flying hours in the Waco, your favorite biplane. Think of it as your graduation present… but I want to talk to you when you return."

Off I went, up over the mountains to one of my favorite spots, the landing strip in the pines at Big Bear Lake. After a short hike with some deep breathing of that fine, pine scented air and a cup of coffee, I took off again. Out over the lake, up over the mountains, reveling in the sheer joy of flying. On the other hand, I was still bothered over what I was going to do with my life. And why did Steve want to talk to me? I soon found out.

Knowing of my average school record on one hand, but noting my excellent attitude and grades on my flying courses, and also aware that my high school grades prohibited college acceptance, he said he knew of a highly respected private aeronautical engineering institute that accepted a high school diploma without reference to grades. They also offered a pre-entrance, home study make-up course tailored to their specific requirements. In turn, they offered a direct path into aircraft design, along with a substantial reputation for placing their graduates as junior engineers with major aircraft firms. The institute provided a highly focused crash course, eight hours a day, five days a week for a year and a half. I was sold. This made sense, though I was a bit nervous over the make-up study course…Now, to persuade my somewhat apprehensive parents.

The school was frightfully expensive and would represent quite a burden on my mom and dad. I couldn't let them down. Having let them down on my earlier schooling, it was most fortunate that they sensed I was truly serious. Indeed, I had finally awakened, and upon my eventual graduation and job placement, they at last had every reason to be proud of me. I loved every minute of the new school, particularly since my primary teacher saw in me an aptitude for design that I was not aware of. He worked patiently with me to bring out this latent aptitude. My life was beginning to have some shape to it. I had attained my private pilot's license through lessons and flying time earned during my hangar sweeping days. I was then taking night school courses in navigation, meteorology and other subjects required for my commercial pilot's license. It was all coming together since I felt that optimum aircraft design ought to be a function of blending engineering knowledge and pilot experience.

The Cal-Aero Technical Institute of Aeronautics was pleased with my performance, and though the catch-up study was back breaking, a new sense of focus had propelled me along. The school was as good as its word and, upon receiving my aeronautical engineering diploma, they placed me with the firm of my choice—North American Aviation.

Soon after settling in on my new job, I started weekend shared-expense flights with friends in order to build up my flying time. These were usually trips between Los Angeles and San Francisco, Las Vegas, Lake Tahoe and Palm Springs.

At this point, I should perhaps confess to an interesting set of flying blunders that occurred on what was to have been an extended vacation flight to the east coast. My friends had relatives there and I was going for the flying. It was to have been a leisurely low altitude survey of our country, stopping wherever we pleased. But it didn't happen that way. Since I had such fierce pride in my flying, the experience I'm about to relate so humiliated me that it left permanently imbedded useful lessons.

On the leg of the flight between Yuma, Arizona and El Paso, Texas, I made a shameful error in navigation. I had not allowed properly for a strong crosswind from the north. After getting hopelessly lost down in Mexico, I decided to use our remaining few gallons of fuel to find a suitable landing spot. This turned out to be a small dry lake bed near a Mexican village.

We were immediately arrested by a pompous but not unkind Chief of Police for not having a visa. A story in itself, which I won't go into here, was dealing with this lack of a visa. This involved wiring the American Consulate in Juarez, on the border with El Paso, and processing the considerable red tape that would allow us to fly north and cross the border into El Paso.

Red tape settled, and after an uncomfortable overnight stay with the airplane, mistake number two was initiated. Mixing with the remaining few gallons of high-octane aviation fuel, I strained enough fuel into the tank from a local gas station to make the flight. As it turned out, their gasoline must have included an element of tequila. On engine run-up, not enough power was produced for me to feel I should try to carry my passengers. I put them on a bus, agreeing to meet them at the El Paso airport.

I took off on a slow climb to the altitude required to clear a low mountain range, leveled off and pondered the engine temperature gage. It was moving inexorably toward the red zone. Having not yet cleared the extremely rough terrain of the mountain range, the engine temperature gage had moved well into the red zone and was still rising. Indeed, I must cool the engine down a bit. As I pulled the throttle to the lowest possible setting without losing altitude, the engine, with no hesitation, instantly seized up... and I sat staring at a frozen propeller!

One is entitled, of course, to a sharp wrench to the gut before getting down to the business of somehow safely executing a forced landing. I had about three thousand feet of altitude over the dry river gulch I was passing at the time—the only possibility in the mountain terrain. But let's not panic, I said to myself. That river gulch had limited straight sections and would require dodging rocks and boulders. It was a last resort and quite possibly would have messed up the airplane and perhaps me too. The very crooked road I was following offered no options at all. Now, a few seconds can be a considerable amount of time to scan for more acceptable alternatives. Such precious seconds are never wasted, and one always has at least ten seconds to scan for alternatives before final commitment to the chosen landing spot.

Looking out ahead, the crooked road wound out of the rough terrain and into a long straight stretch. Could I make it?...What was my glide ratio with a frozen non-idling engine. I didn't know. But my now stabilized glide showed a rate of descent which, even in my then limited judgement of such things, suggested I could perhaps just barely stretch my glide onto the straight stretch of road. Yes, I could make it.

Flying in a canyon the last part of the glide, I swung out onto the straightaway with a couple of hundred feet of altitude to spare... enough altitude to note a truck moving away from me about a mile down the scarcely traveled road, and to note puffs of dust blowing across the road from my left. I had just enough altitude to increase my glide speed a bit and assure line-up on the narrow high banked road and to correct for the cross wind. I wasn't quite home free just yet. I had never used so narrow a runway, confined by the steep banks to each side. Correcting for drift, favoring the left side of the road, I sat her down. More left brake and careening perilously close to the right side bank, I came to a stop...Thank you, God.

I sat quietly for a few minutes, blocking whatever traffic might come along next, and then got out of the airplane just as a farm truck pulled up from the rear. Drawing on my feeble high school Spanish, the Mexican farmer graciously helped me push the airplane down the road to a turnout.

Now, what was the biggest lesson here? That is, other than my stupid navigational error and the attempted use of questionable fuel. The biggest lesson was to build upon the idea of situational "scanning."

In the above forced landing situation, I must have been subconsciously "scanning" since, after the engine failed, I was seriously considering doing my best with the dry river gulch. Those few seconds of alternative consideration, setting aside panic and a strong tendency to over-concentrate on the gulch, were those precious seconds that led to casting the decision in the right direction.

Returning now to that lonely Mexican road, with the airplane pushed out of the way on a turnout, what next? Among other things, large lessons in social and bureaucratic interface. I should like to share a most unusual situation in this regard, one that I've often described to myself as "angel intervention."

So, here is this twenty-one year old kid, namely me, standing on the edge of the road wondering what to do next. The first order of business was to somehow protect a very expensive airplane that did not belong to me. While pondering this, a police patrol car pulled up. The patrolman seemed somewhat confused as to how to deal with the situation.

Then, the mystery "angel" appeared. A middle-aged Mexican wearing a black, double-breasted, pin-striped suit, tie and a homburg hat, pulled up in an old Chevrolet coupe. He said nothing to me. He turned to the patrolman and even though he spoke kindly, there was no mistaking the quiet authority in his tone. They finished their dialogue in Spanish and the patrolman called someone on his radio, then said to me in poor English, "I guard airplane."

My homburg-hatted angel, still not saying a word to me, motioned me to get in his car. Why should I trust this strange apparition, appearing out of nowhere on this lonely road? But an intuitive feeling said go with him. Still not saying a word, we pulled up in front of what appeared to be a military garrison of some sort.

We were immediately received by the officer in charge and after a dialogue in Spanish between my angel and the officer, the officer turned to me and said in English: "We will put an overnight guard on your airplane and until you can make arrangements with the American Consulate. I will call and advise them of the situation. Good luck to you."

I thanked him and once again we were back in the angel's Chevrolet. Still not one word to me. The next thing I knew, we were in front of the American Consulate. I thanked him profusely. He then said the only words he had spoken to me in all the time we had been together. Tuning his unsmiling but very kind face to me and tipping his homburg hat, he said: "Via con Dios", (Go with God). With that, he drove off and I never saw him again.

Entering the American Consulate in Juarez, I was graciously met by the man in charge, George Henderson. The first thing he did was to drive me back out to the airplane in order to assure that, indeed, it was safe and properly guarded for the night. He then drove me to the El Paso airport to seek out a mechanic and to arrange for tools, aviation fuel and an oil change. Mr. Henderson said to go ahead and cross the border the next morning with the mechanic and materials. He would make all the arrangements for this including the clearance for take off and the short flight to the El Paso airport—that is, if the airplane proved flyable. The horrendous expense of dismantling the airplane and trucking it across the border was simply unthinkable if at all avoidable.

He then took me to an early dinner and dropped me off at a motel next to the airport. I would ride out with the mechanic in the morning. What a totally gracious experience to be treated so kindly during my obvious distress over my stupidity in getting myself into such a mess.

The next morning we gathered our materials and drove in the mechanic's truck down to the airplane. We drained the tequila-based fuel and put in ten gallons of high-octane aviation fuel. We drained the oil, noting with some concern the number of metal fragments in it, put in fresh oil and new spark plugs. I fired up the engine. On stationary run-up, it ran terribly rough but seemed to produce the power required for takeoff. Without enough information to properly assess the length of time the engine would hold up, I somewhat arbitrarily decided the engine should be good enough for the ten or fifteen minute flight to the El Paso airport.

The road was cleared and after a much longer takeoff run than I had anticipated, the airplane reluctantly became airborne. Leaving wing flaps slightly extended for better lift, bluish-white smoke pouring out of the exhaust stacks, engine horribly rough, struggling for altitude not much higher than tree top level, the short flight to the El Paso airport was successfully completed... another big sigh of relief as the airplane was pushed into a nice, secure American hangar.

We tore down the engine immediately, finding such degeneration of pistons that we wondered at the engine running at all. We immediately shipped the engine to Los Angeles for a rush rebuild job. Service was very good and we got the engine back in ten days.

In the meantime, my friends decided to continue their vacation trip on the bus and I had a quite pleasant stay in El Paso. I was wonderfully treated by George Henderson and his wife, who involved me socially at the American Consulate after all the fuss was over. The airport crew also provided new friends. I spent some of the time writing a lengthy article on the experience for a flying magazine, which they accepted and paid for; and which at least helped a bit in defraying expenses.

This particular story ends quietly as the engine was promptly returned and installed and the flight back to Los Angeles uneventful. A happy footnote to my return was the attitude of the people of the flying service from whom I had rented an expensive new airplane. I had assumed they would no longer be my friends. But with their airplane back in their hangar, good as new, they were most appreciative of my responsible attitude in seeing to its proper return. They were better friends than ever... It was a while, however, before I was able to pay off the bank loan required to cover the rebuilding of the engine. But nonetheless mighty happy that it all worked out well, leaving deeply imbedded, lasting lessons.

And now that my job was secure and was paying merit increases in salary every six months, it was time to enter into that most important event in my life—marriage. Even though shy around the girls and having done very little dating, I had the extreme good fortune to meet a very lovely girl who just had to be the one for me. After sharing a beautiful relationship for a couple of years, we found our love for each other to be quite solid. Hence, on August 30, 1941, we were married in a little church in the romantic town of Montecito, just south of the coastal city of Santa Barbara.

Notwithstanding the adjustments to be made in any marriage—particularly when a smart, levelheaded girl marries a maverick—my marriage to Rosemary has been a lasting and productive one.

However, only a few months after we were married, that infamous date of December Seventh reared its head—the Japanese attack on Pearl Harbor and the declaration of war.

In my own case, I had a wartime draft exempt position as an engineer with an aircraft company producing military airplanes. But I also had at this point my commercial pilot's license. The demand for pilots was soaring to new levels.

While I consider myself to be a very patriotic person, I also harbored a secret desire to test my flying skills under conditions as extreme as I could find. Little did I realize at the time just how extreme that challenge would turn out to be.

There were options: Airline copilot with progression to airline captain; civilian flight school instructor; or the Air Force Air Transport Command. Pondering these options, I called my old flight instructor friend, Steve, who had just joined the ATC as a civilian pilot. He was very enthused since the primary mission of the ATC at that time was ferrying all types of fighter, bomber and transport aircraft all over the United States and the world. Steve pointed out that civilian pilots could only fly in the U.S.A., but that after a period of time the civilian pilots would be directly commissioned as Air Force officers and fly to destinations all over the world. That sounded great to me.

Commercial pilot license in hand, I gathered up my logbooks of flying hours and drove to the ATC base in Long Beach, California to apply for a civilian pilot position. However, this was not at first a happy process. In applying to the Air Force colonel who was running the civilian pilot hiring program, my still somewhat fragile confidence took a temporary beating. This particular colonel was a pompous, ungracious snothead. More that that, he was and old man. Must have been damn near forty. He looked at this twenty-three year old kid with a grimace, disdainfully flipped through my pitiful log books full of only light plane flying time and, in his imperious manner, turned to one of his lieutenants and said: "Lieutenant, take this kid out and see if he can drive an airplane."

The flight test was another matter. The very gracious lieutenant assigned to my test said: "Don't pay any attention to old iron pants. Let's go have some fun." I was now at ease. He put me in the front cockpit of an Air Force advanced trainer with its 650 horsepower engine, twice the horsepower of anything I had previously flown, and we were off into the blue. My confidence was back and I happily executed the routines he asked for, terminating the flight with a smooth landing in an aircraft I had not flown before. He congratulated me on a well executed flight and reported same to the colonel. While I do believe the colonel's expression bordered on disappointment, I was hired.

First assignments were as copilot on bomber flights. We were not a part of a regular crew. We flew with various airplane commanders as our names were called from a rotational card file. I didn't like this aspect one bit. Most of the time I drew excellent pilots who were there to get the job done. At other times I drew hot-doggers—pilots who had too much fun buzzing small towns on the deck, flying down canyons or harassing and buzzing slower airplanes.

I recall one terribly tragic incident, which I viewed from a trailing distance in another airplane. It seems this particular hot-dogger had elected to tease a slower American Airlines DC-3. He was crossing back and forth over the airliner. On about the third crossover, he misjudged his distance and ripped the tail off the airliner. The airliner immediately spun in and all were killed.

The hot-dogger's bomber, however, experienced only one disabled engine and he was able to land at the nearest airport. Obviously, his life and career were over… but over. Most sadly, he was a likeable, nice guy. I do not know what eventually happened to him as he was immediately transferred away from our base. His poor, unwitting copilot was so shaken that he was grounded for psychiatric treatment.

In talking with my friend, Steve, about my dislike of this random hot-dogging business, he asked if I were aware of one of the ATC policies for new pilots in which options were offered as to flight assignments. No one had mentioned the following option to me: New civilian pilots had the option of riding copilot for six months and then transitioning as twin engine airplane commanders... or, new pilots could fly solo in fighter aircraft for six months and then transition directly as multi-engine airplane commanders. Guess what? I just about broke a leg getting to the operations officer and signing up for fighter aircraft.

Fighter transition was real fun. The instructor first put me into the cockpit of a single seat P-51 Mustang, a favorite of mine produced by my former company—North American Aviation. He told me what to expect as to the airplane's flight characteristics, cautioning me to expect very heavy right rudder application on the initial part of the takeoff run in order to overcome the torque of the P-51's powerful engine. He then pointed out all the switches, instruments, levers and fuel distribution management valves, patted me on the back and said: "Have a nice flight." It wasn't nice at all... it was simply great! Moreover, I was on my own. No more hot-doggers.

After a reasonably good landing in this hot little number, I wanted to take the rest of the day off and revel in the joy of it. "Oh no", laughed the instructor. "Let's go down the line here and check you out in the P-40. Then tomorrow we'll do the P-47 Thunderbolt and the P-39 Aircobra." Talk about a kid in a candy store. I had a ball. After three or four days of local practice flying in these four fighter aircraft, I was ready for ferrying assignments.

I flew fighters to bases on just about every corner of the U.S.A. with a wonderful sense of freedom, doing my own conservative hot-dogging. While I never, but never harassed other airplanes or startled sleepy towns, I had a nodding acquaintance with more than one railroad engineer. I must say I enjoyed seeing most of the open country, lakes and rivers of the U.S.A. from an average altitude of about one hundred feet... beautiful!

On ferrying new airplanes, we were not allowed to fly on instruments or at night, thus minimizing the risk of possible post-production problems on airplanes fresh off the assembly line. For example, on one occasion I picked up a new P-51 and, unknown to me on takeoff, the landing gear retracted, but the wheel fairing doors did not close. On my first planned stop at Tucson, Arizona, I couldn't get a green gear-down light on both main wheels. The control tower informed me that my landing gear was only partly extended. A bit nervous about this, I climbed to about three thousand feet, entered a shallow dive and pulled up smartly. Gravity snapped the gear into place. Reassuringly green lights appeared on the instrument panel for an uneventful landing.

After taxiing to the flight line, I opened the engine cowling and guess what? There was no cap on the hydraulic fluid reservoir, only an oily rag hanging out of it. On takeoff, there must have been just enough juice to partially retract the gear. It all worked out O.K., but there were always "the little things" to be on guard for.

The pilot discretion we had on our flights was good. If we encountered weather, it was up to the pilot to decide whether or not he could maintain visual flight rules or return to the nearest airport. Each night we were required to send a Remaining-Overnight wire to home base Flight Operations Control. Happily, if one had a good reputation, unusual stops were not challenged by the home base operations officer.

I recall one happy incident over Nebraska on my way to Omaha when the weather ahead looked threatening but which might or might not permit continuing to visual flight rules. I elected to return early in the afternoon to the civilian airport in North Platte. As it so happened, smiling smugly to myself, my grandparents' farm was not too many miles north of the airport. After my gracious civilian hosts rolled the P-51 into the United Airlines hangar for the night, I went next door to a flying service and hired a pilot to fly me to grandfather's farm in his Piper cub—a light plane with oversize wheels for landing on unimproved fields.

Not having seen my grandparents for many years, they were, of course, taken completely by surprise. I had a very pleasant evening with them and my uncle along with a wonderful dinner of wild pheasant and a deep feather bed. It was like rolling the calendar back. Nothing had changed, not even the outdoor privy on that cold November night, nor the hand pump in the kitchen for well water or the wood stove to heat the water for a bath… ahhh, yes.

The next morning dawned bright and beautiful. My favorite uncle offered to drive me to the North Platte airport. Great. Leaving at dawn, we had a good visit, arriving at the airport around the middle of the day. As a country farmer, he was thrilled and proud as I put him in the cockpit of the P-51 for a tour of my flying machine. Shortly thereafter, on the end of the runway, ready for takeoff, I asked the control tower's permission to give the airport a high speed buzz on the deck… A friendly, "Permission granted" from the tower. A final salute to my dear uncle, who I never saw again.

All in all, flying single engine fighters of all types for six months occurred with relatively few scares. The aircraft factory production people actually did quite a remarkable job and caused not too much trouble in some of their final inspection oversights. The biggest problem for those of us flying all types of aircraft on irregular flight schedules—particularly those who were flying the single cockpit twin engine aircraft—were the frightful variations in cockpit design.

We really had to watch ourselves in dealing with these wide variations in the arrangement of instruments, switches, warning lights, landing gear handle shape and placement, wing flaps handle shape and placement, the arrangement of throttles, propeller pitch control, propeller feathering buttons, propeller deicing fluid controls, fuel mixture controls, carburetor heat controls, trim tab dials for rudder, elevator and ailerons, auto pilot control, location of fuel distribution valves, oxygen system valve, emergency fire controls, emergency air brake control, radio navigation system and communication system controls, etc., etc.

The point is: While the cockpit is, in effect, a rather complex flying office, it was also necessary to look outside from time to time to see where the hell one was going, not to mention navigation and response to air traffic control.

Inordinate preoccupation with cockpit idiosyncrasies, when yielded to, often caused serious problems. Sadly, accidents and even fatal crashes occurred through improper reckoning both with cockpit variables from airplane type to airplane type as well as less than optimum cockpit design in any individual type of airplane. The pilot admonition always was: Know thy cockpit! Know it to a point of automatic reaction to whatever the particular operational need.

A wisecracking Air Force test pilot, in a formal cockpit evaluation report, sarcastically congratulated the Cockpit Standardization Committee on their "fine work." He pointed out that in all the various cockpit designs he had flown, the pilot actually face forward. Period! There is a not so subtle point here that I shall share in later chapters in some depth. It is this: The communications between military operational specifications writers and the aircraft industry designers who are supposed to respond to these specifications was very weak and even today is not yet as strong as it ought to be. They used to call the design process of pilot accommodation "Human Engineering." Now a more esoteric term is used. The call it "Ergonomics"... and that new term isn't getting the job done either, to the degree that it should... More later.

So, for now, on to multi-engine aircraft flight transition to airplane commander in all types, starting with the C-47, B-25, B-26, A-20, P-38, P-61 and later, the A-26. Qualifying in all these highly variable types indeed kept one's head on full alert. My wife was bemused by the extensive library of operations manuals on my bedside table which were studied far into the night... well, not always... My wife cheerfully referred to these manuals as my "other wives", but was quick to endorse their importance.

These airplanes, of course, were quite different from one another. The C-47 (DC-3), for example, handled like a butterfly in comparison to the hotter airplanes. On the other end of the spectrum of various types, our flight school also had an early model of the stub wing B-26 that we referred to as the "Rock With Fins." That bomber handled hot and heavy. The designers finally admitted to this and later models exhibited the proper amount of wingspread. But whether light or heavy-handling single, twin or four engine airplane, it may also be interesting to bring out a very subtle characteristic common to all types of airplanes—particularly when piloting a mix of all types at irregular intervals. It was not always easy to teach, but every airplane has "its own voice." That is to say, the airplane will "tell the pilot" what it wants if the pilot schools himself to remain sensitive to "what the airplane is saying to him." If the pilot does not "listen" to subtle or sometimes not so subtle variations in aircraft behavior, he tends to force-fit the different flight characteristics into his preconceived notion of how the aircraft ought to behave, rather than listen to "the voice" of the airplane... and every type of airplane has its own voice.

Many ferrying flights were made in these various airplane types which, among other things, brought out some of "the little things" in design which can kill or seriously injure a pilot. I recall one instance with a single cockpit, twin engine attack bomber—the Douglas A-20.

First, note that most all air-cooled engines have a single switch to open or close engine cowl flaps. These are gills on the trailing edge of the engine cowling that must be kept wide open for proper engine temperature control while on the ground. The last procedural step before takeoff is to close the engine cowl flaps. In the case of the A-20, unlike other types, it had two cowl flap switches—one for lower flaps and one for upper flaps on top of the wing. If a pilot tried to take off without closing the upper flaps on a hot desert day, the airplane simply would not fly because the upper cowl flaps acted as wing lift spoilers.

I had picked up a new A-20 at a desert processing base in Barstow, California. It was a 100-degree day. I started down the hot desert runway in this fully loaded A-20 and at full power rolled and rolled on my ground run. But I wasn't flying! I should have been airborne. The end of the runway was looming. Too late to abort the takeoff without crashing into the rough terrain just off the end... Thank you dear guardian angel! A big bright light went on in my brain and the brain said, "Hey, Dummy, you forgot to close the top cowl flaps." I quickly flipped the switch and the A-20 flew, barely clearing the boundary fence at the end of the runway.

There are many such design traps for the pilot in various types of aircraft. Ben Howard, Douglas Aircraft test pilot, called these sorts of things "open elevator shafts." A good analogy. I later phoned him on the top cowl flap problem and he immediately came up with a quick fix: Spring load the top cowl flaps so that if the pilot forgets to flip the second switch, the air stream will blow them closed... neat!

In addition to ferrying flights in the twin engine airplanes, I was also given my flight transition checkout on the four engine B-17 Flying Fortress and the B-24 Liberator. This completed the requirements for my Air Force "Five P" pilot rating, which authorized my flying as airplane commander to any part of the world in any type of aircraft operated by the U.S. Air Force.

At this point in my tenure with the Air Transport Command, having scored rather well with the transition flight instructors, I was recruited as one of them myself in the twin engine flight transition school. However, before activating me as flight instructor, I was advised it was first appropriate to change me from civilian pilot to Air Force officer. Pouring "military holy water" on me was an unexpectedly quick process. Along with other candidates, I was hustled down to the firing range to qualify as marksman with the 45 automatic pistol, marched around the parade field in drill formation a few times, given a short ground school in military protocol... and, wha-da-ya know, I was "anointed" as an Air Force officer.

A side point to all of the above, which to this day continues to amuse me, is this: The Air Force military hierarchy, in their great, caste-structured wisdom, decided that while they had "anointed" the civilian pilots as full-fledged military officers, they should somehow brand us with some kind of social stain which would differentiate those pilots who were Air Force Cadet School graduates from those of us who came to the Air Force from less postured civilian flying schools—those of us from the wrong side of the tracks, so to speak.

Therefore, we were suitably branded by being directed to wear a big "S" on our wings, designating us as Service Pilots, whatever that meant. Being a maverick civilian at heart, I was as annoyed with that "S" brand as I was with certain aspects of the military's caste system between officers and enlisted men.

However, the whole "S" brand concept eventually backfired on the Air Force hierarchy and fell apart. It seemed that too many of those of us with "S" brands on our wings were moving into vital command and flight instructor positions over Air Force cadet school graduates who, in many cases, though good pilots, couldn't cut it as flight instructors or as operations commanders in various management roles. Hence, a new policy. With a stroke of the base commander's pen, I was no longer branded a Service Pilot. I was "made pure" and the "S" stigma removed from my wings. Removing the "S" brand was not mandatory and many service pilots didn't bother to apply for a changeover. In my own case, I could see a certain political utility in going with the flow.

Now, back to the fun part. As flight instructor in the twin engine school, I entered a whole new phase of learning about flying. (Don't tell my students.) Using the B-25 as our mainstay trainer, extensive instructor time was invested in training pilots to emergency single engine procedures on twin engine airplanes in the event of failure of one engine. With students, this was touchy business. While the B-25 was a fine airplane, it commanded a great deal of respect when operating with one engine out. Students were taught emergency propeller feathering procedures at cruising altitude, the instructor always chopping the left or right engine when the student least expected it. The idea was to measure the student's quickness of response to the requirement for immediately applying heavy rudder into live engine before the asymmetrical power from the live engine rolled the airplane over toward the dead engine. With the initial aspect of single engine operation in hand, the student was evaluated on a combination of speed and error-free deliberation on all other accompanying procedures: applying extra power and related propeller pitch on the live engine; pushing the propeller feathering button on the dead engine, of course, not the live engine as was often the tendency in the early phase of training; the dead engine ignition shutdown; and, lastly, redistribution-fuel-valve management.

The flight instructor had to maintain extra diligence not only because of the B-25's touchy behavior, but to be a good instructor he had to be able to allow the student to go as far as he dared into a correctable mistake in single engine procedure. For example, making turns into the dead engine with high power on the live engine was a decided "no-no." If not quickly stopped, rollover was a distinct possibility.

The next step in the training was single engine landings. Unlike single engine operation at cruising altitude, single engine landings required a high degree of final commitment. With landing gear and full wing flaps extended, depending on aircraft loading, it was all too easy to make a missed approach decision too late to retract gear and flaps, reestablish airplane trim and bring back the necessary power to go around again without running out of air space. Parenthetically, I should note that while we taught full engine shutdown and propeller feathering at cruising altitude, safety considerations in the single engine landing situation dictated that the "dead engine" be kept in idle power, ready to go... just in case.

The scanning rule was also very important in the one engine failure situation. To each student, it was underscored that while immediate heavy rudder into the good engine following engine failure was a must, all other procedures were to be allowed a few seconds of deliberation. The admonition to the student was: "Don't get smart and show off an ability to go too quickly through a complex procedure. No matter how capable a pilot you are, use those few extra seconds to truly get it right—should a gut-wrenching real emergency confront you. Training is one thing, the real emergency is quite another!"

Now, we repeat all of the above training at night, since the ATC was by then getting into night flying to foreign destinations after seasoning the new airplane and it's commander in local flights. As it was, my own previous night flying time had been limited to a few hours of light plane time. I was hesitant to mention this to the operations officer due, I suppose, to a bit of false pride. Hence, I was handed a roster of night students and told to grab a B-25 and go to it. Needless to say, I learned a great deal more about flying on this night training caper and wound up with an intense night flying background, which was to serve me well on things to come.

In the night flying training situation, the weeding out process alone was a growth experience for me. Some students who were passable under daylight training conditions, simply backed off in the night flying training situation, admitting they were not yet ready for the airplane commander's seat. Usually, they made fine copilots. Ascertaining this lack of readiness by some students exacted inordinate care and alertness on the part of the transition instructor, since every effort was made not to compromise the student's career. And so, training life went on.

After a few months of intense day and night flight instructor work, I found myself wanting to offer the operations officer a few suggestions on management of the twin engine school. Lt. Col. Sam Dunlap was a good listener.

As noted, the B-25 was our mainstay transition trainer. We had only four B-25's, and yet the demand for more twin engine airplane commanders was growing very rapidly. Our trainer airplanes took a terrible beating. The bulk of the training not only involved occasional hard student landings, but as many as five or six touch-and-go landings per hour, fully cycling all mechanical systems in the process. Breakdowns were frequent, along with the scares often accompanying them. Maintaining increasing flight schedules was fast becoming impossible.

I suggested that in order to fly an average twelve to fourteen hours per day per airplane on day and night training schedules, we needed at least nine B-25 airplanes in order to keep three in the air. Col. Dunlap thought this number a bit high, but I had roughly confirmed this in discussions with my former colleagues at North American Aviation—producers of the B-25 airplane. The operations officer was sold, along with his acceptance of several new training procedures, the need for which were exposed during a few close calls with students in my flight instructor activities.

I went about my normal day and night instructor duties only to get a call from the operations officer a couple of weeks later in which he advised me that I was to head the twin engine flight transition school. Admittedly, I was flattered by this assignment and at the same time amused over his smiling remark to the effect that he was glad they had removed the "S" brand on my wings, since I would be directing the training activities of both civilian service pilots and Air Force Cadet School graduates... A nonsense point. I gave him my best maverick smirk and got on with it.

I'm grateful to report that the next few months proceeded quite intensely but, all in all, quite smoothly with relatively few close calls, thanks to the fine support of the operations office, my guardian angel and a superb cadre of flight instructors—Frank Moore, Fred Kuster, Court Remele, Bill Willoghby, Rex Lamar, Joe Wisdom and others. We broke records on the graduation of twin engine pilots without a single injury accident.

Moving toward the close of this early years summary, there arrived on our base the gleaming new Douglas Aircraft A-26 twin engine attack bomber. The company pilot had left it on our flight line along with a copy of the operations manual. I could hardly wait. Sitting in the single cockpit of this large twin engine beauty, I quietly read the operations manual for an hour or so, and then proceeded to check myself out in flight. While it had a few small problems, and its landing characteristics were somewhat different from other twin engine types, it flew like a dream.

Because of my engineering background, I suppose, I was loaned to Douglas Aircraft for some cross-country fuel consumption tests on this new airplane. Since first deliveries of the A-26 were to the Air Force operational base in Shreveport, Louisiana, we used normal ferrying flights for the fuel consumption tests. A month or so of these tests and the Air Force decided that although there were still a few development bugs to be worked out, this was a wartime situation and it was time to send the first of the A-26's to an operational combat group in war torn England. This was in the early summer of 1944. Guess who got this assignment? My flight was followed by three others, giving the operational group in England the first nucleus of a new combat capability.

Closing this chapter on the early years of an eighty year odyssey, it seemed appropriate to share with the reader the fact that we all have God-given talents which, for one reason or another, may remain hidden. Hidden, that is, until some circumstance, or a more perceptive viewpoint by someone in a higher position brings these latent talents to one's attention.

For example, my unexpected appointment as head of the twin engine flight transition school was my very first encounter with significant managerial responsibility. Thanks to a few supportive people in my background, this assignment seemed to be a perfectly natural thing for me to do—putting a number of complex considerations into a semblance of order and then seeing that they were carried out. My maverick tendency, probably, and a hint of entrepreneurial aptitude accounted for much of this, although I hadn't nailed down that line of reasoning at the time.

Finally, I must underscore that prayer had a great deal to do with whatever I was involved in. Yes, stumbling at times for not always listening to His words of wisdom, but always finding a patient God on hand to pick me up again. I also tried hard to make use of my maverickness without letting it run away with me... again, not always succeeding. Awakening from uncertainty, lack of self confidence and, finally, "going for it"—particularly if one is also a maverick—finds one all the more dependent on God's presence and, as best he can, listening to His guardian angels... or, if one prefers, listening to intuition, a God-given derivative for blending spiritual guidance with practical issues.

Moving on, then, to the most dangerous years of this odyssey and the poignant lessons they offered.

Chapter Three
The Poignancy and Lessons of Hazardous Flight
India, Tibet, China, Burma, South China Sea

On a sultry hot day in August, 1944, we arrived at our Air Force ATC base in the steamy jungles of Northern Assam Valley, India near the small town of Jorhat on the great Brhamaputra River. This base was located at the foot of the treacherous Himalayas, over which we soon would be flying.

After settling us in our respective grass-roofed bash huts, we were given a tour of the base. At that time of its remarkable short-term development, it was a little city in its own right. It was home to several hundred pilots and air crew members, together with hundreds of support personnel and a large complement of cargo-converted B-24 Liberators—the total number varying with lost aircraft and crews and their rates of replacement.

Then, before flight assignments, we were given several indoctrination lectures. These lectures by seasoned Hump pilots dove right into the facts of Himalayan Hump flying. At that point in time, our base, together with other Hump flying bases, had already experienced hundreds, yes, hundreds of fatal aircraft losses, multiplied by a crew of four for each aircraft lost! It was difficult to digest this aspect of Hump flying. Was it really *that* dangerous?

All of this was further aggravated by radical, risk increasing changes in Hump flying policies. When the extremely hazardous idea of flying supplies from India to China over more than five

50

hundred miles of the most formidable mountains in the world, not to mention some routes over enemy held territory, flights were permitted only during daylight hours and with some deference toward bad weather.

By the time I arrived for Hump duty, the number of missions required to complete a tour of duty had doubled. Moreover, a new ATC commanding general, swiveling smartly in his desk chair at ATC Division Headquarters in Calcutta, decreed that the Hump would never be closed. Round the clock, twenty-four-hours-a-day, with no Hump flying shutdown due to weather... Wow! Did that new policy ever cost an increase in lost lives.

As a patriotic American who damn well knew there was a war going on, and that high risk was the name of the game, I still wondered, at first, where a cost-effectiveness study might fit in— particularly in the light of the hundreds of aircraft and crews already lost. That is to say, there is no doubt that the logistic contribution by the Hump flying operation played a significant role in furnishing the supplies needed to help shorten the war. But was there some point of balance between lives lost on the supplier side and the gains made by the consumers of those supplies? I came to agree with myself that this was an imponderable question.

So, we got on with the increased risk and, all in all, performed a massive logistic task for which we can remain forever proud.

Our next indoctrination lecture was on jungle survival procedures. We were shown how to use the survival kit strapped to our parachute harness. It contained mini shotgun shells for use in our automatic pistol for small game hunting, fishhooks and line, dried food and limited first aid supplies. A separate money belt was strapped on for each flight in the event we should be faced with an emergency bail out. This was to furnish us with a bartering medium in seeking the natives' help in finding our way out from wherever the bail out found us. While many bailouts were lost forever, a surprising number of bailouts successfully walked out—sometimes many weeks later.

In that same lecture on emergency bail out, it was underscored that if any possibility existed to stay with the airplane until at the lower altitudes or over the jungle areas, that was preferable to bailing out over the high mountains with the most likely probability of landing on a fifteen to twenty-thousand foot slope. With standard issue Air Force parachute—not a para-glider by any means—landing in the rarefied atmosphere of those altitudes could involve fatal injury or incapacitation… Cheerful prospect!

Then, the final lecture on navigation, which was the aircraft commander's responsibility. We did not have navigators. Our crew consisted of pilot, copilot, flight engineer and a vitally important, long distance radio operator. The lecturer described the far northern route over Tibet to our operational B-29 bases in Chengtu, China, to which we carried one of our primary cargos, fuel for the B-29s. He then described the still high but more navigable mountain routes to the south on our Kunming, China, cargo deliveries. We were also advised of the few emergency landing fields at LiChiang on the northern route, Yunnanyi on the middle route and Myitkyina on the most southerly route. We were advised that the Myitkyina base had only recently been recaptured from the Japanese and that occasional snipers were still being smoked out. The lecturer also advised us of the still held enemy territory on the southerly route, some in the vicinity of the Burma Road. We were further advised that while on the southerly routes at night, all aircraft navigation and cabin lights were to be turned off in order to preclude Japanese night fighter attacks. He didn't mention what to do during daylight flights. No good answer, probably. Additional points, the lecturer said, would be covered during our indoctrination flights. "Welcome to the Hump," he closed, "Good flying."

Those of us who came to the Hump with Five-P pilot ratings were given one indoctrination flight as copilot and then checked immediately by the chief pilot or one of his assistants. Was I ready for this? I deeply hoped so.

My indoctrination flight as copilot to Dick Carpenter, a good pilot friend from Long Beach, California, was a fairly smooth daylight flight with a minimum of bad weather on the somewhat lower altitude middle route to Kunming. He gave me many good pointers on what to expect.

My check out flight in the airplane commander's seat by the much-respected chief pilot was a real taste of what it was all about. Our Air Traffic Control clearance was on the far northern route over Tibet to Chengtu, taking off for a mostly daylight trip and then returning at night. My instrument flying got a full inspection through a very heavy dose of vicious thunderstorm activity and an instrument approach to a low ceiling in Chengtu. The return flight was not so bad, but again involved a low ceiling instrument approach to Jorhat at night. I asked the chief pilot if the vicious thunderstorm we had passed through was as bad as it gets. He half-smiled and said, "I don't want to unduly alarm you, but, no, that was not as bad as it gets. All of us are always waiting for the Really Big One. Some of those who hit the Really Big One didn't make it. Some did."

In any case, I was approved as a flight commander and immediately put on rotational call for flight. That is, there were no schedules for pilots. One reported to the flight line as an aircraft became available, loaded and ready to go.

With the nonscheduled system, even as a young man, I recall how difficult it often was to find one's self dozing off to sleep for the night at nine or ten o'clock—after having returned from a mission earlier that same day—and then having one's shoulder shaken by the flight caller who often, in a sympathetic tone of voice, said, "Call for flight, Captain." One then struggled to get up out of the sack, pull one's head together, and then fly all night... Ahhh, youth.

My first few flights as airplane commander went fairly smoothly with only moderately scary weather. Then, my first really hairy emergency. We were on the far northern route at night at twenty-five thousand feet, with our usual several-ton overload, augmented by an increasing load of ice. As earlier noted, we had no wing deicer system, only propeller anti-icing fluid. We had just increased power to deal with the icing condition when number three propeller pitch control went into an uncontrollable surge back and forth from low pitch to high pitch. The nonsynchronous sound against the synchronous drone of the other three engines was in itself disconcerting. We wondered how long it would hold up before causing an engine shut down. Then, a most unexpected additional event added to our emergency. With no warning whatsoever, number four engine coughed a couple of times and suddenly quit cold. The propeller was immediately feathered and still more power added to engines one and two as well as the surging number three engine. This was, indeed, a very tight spot. In no way could we immediately descend below our twenty-five thousand-foot minimum instrument altitude. We had only recently passed LiChiang with its nearby twenty-three thousand foot peaks.

We were still in solid cloud cover on instruments. The Air Force base at Yunnanyi looked like our best chance to avoid the dreaded bail out. I estimated we were about one hundred miles due north of Yunnanyi with its surrounding mountain peaks at fifteen thousand feet. We turned due south with an estimated twenty degree course correction to account for strong westerly winds. With full power on three engines, we were barely holding altitude, realizing that once the engine temperature gauges soared into the red zone, power would have to be reduced. With copilot Bob Carmichael watching the temperature gauges, I directed Pete Kanoff, my radio operator, to send out an S.O.S. and to advise Yunnanyi operations of our plan. I then directed Pete and flight engineer Ted Bain to dump our cargo as quickly as possible.

During the cargo dumping process, we got a real break. Our guardian angel hadn't forgotten us after all. We burst out of our cloud cover into bright, full moonlight. We could now see the mountain tops scooting under our fannies. Bob called my attention to the engine temperature gauges and I immediately cut back on the power, now that I could see what we were dealing with. We still had our wing ice, but Pete and Ted had jettisoned the cargo door and were frantically dumping cargo within the few minutes available on their walk-around oxygen bottles. I could feel our descent rate flattening and we were starting to lose our wing ice.

Turning my attention back to navigation, I tuned our radio compass to the Yunnanyi beacon—in most cases, the only radio navigation aid available to us. The only problem was that the compass needle danced wildly in full moonlight and would settle down on the beacon only when very close to the station. On moonless nights, the needle would hold steady on a beacon at a considerable distance. I've never had an explanation of that phenomenon. But that was the way of it—moonlight and a view of what was going on, or no moon and a steady radio compass needle with no outside reference. We always watched our magnetic compass navigation carefully, but on night flights we were almost entirely dependent on the radio compass for properly securing our destination. While I had made a rough calculation of the required compass heading to Yunnanyi from the estimated point where the emergency had occurred, and was reasonably sure our new compass heading was correct, I was still anxious to see our swinging radio compass needle settle down and confirm this.

Now, if number three engine would hold up for another half hour or so, we would be O.K. I should note that while an empty B-24 will fly with two engines out on one side, it's a real bitch to handle if any kind of turbulence is involved. So far, we were getting a break on that score. Since leaving our instrument flight condition, the air was reasonably smooth. With cargo dumped and wing ice decreasing we were going to make it. We could now deal precisely with the mountain peaks in the clear moonlight.

While anxiously peering through the windshield after nearly half an hour on our emergency course, a most heartwarming sight greeted our eyes—the beacon and runway lights of Yunnanyi. My compass heading was off just a few degrees to the east, not having allowed quite enough course correction for the prevailing westerly wind. With Yunnanyi enjoying clear weather, we executed our two-and-a-half-engine landing without incident. Big sighs of relief all around and my own private, "Thank you, God".... Powdered eggs, toast and coffee never tasted so good!

My crew and I were picked up the next day by a Jorhat airplane returning empty from Kunming. A couple of days on the ground and we were back on rotational schedule.

As a general comment, one eventually reached a point where, though still waiting for the Really Big One, fear was kept at bay and he could take in and actually enjoy the magnificent once-in-a-lifetime experience he was involved in... much of the time. On a pre-dawn flight to Kunming, for example, arriving just as the first rays of the sun started painting the dawn mists and cliffs of Kunming's beautiful Lake Tien-Chi-Hi, offering a spectrum of magical blends of color like no other.

The mountain city of Kunming itself, at 6,500-foot altitude, also had its charms. China even smelled differently—not bad, just different. From time to time, there were opportunities to walk about the city, which I always did, no matter what country I was visiting. On the perimeter of Kunming were the usual pockets of poverty, as found in most areas of the world. But Kunming, a mere village then, held a particular charm as one walked through the center of town in the evening. It had a candlelight and lantern warmth and charm to it. One evening, my crew and I stopped at, of all things, a hat and gong shop. We tried on coolie hats and tested all the gongs, much to the joy and laughter of the shopkeeper and his family as well as the passers-by. Even with a war going on, there was a certain element of smiles and laughter among many of the Chinese people we encountered.

Then, there were those night flights in quiet, clear air, passing one of the widely spread Tibetan monasteries, built in great isolation at incredible altitudes. There were often torch processions, zigzagging on high mountain trails. What did they mean? It didn't matter. One could embrace a dream-like magic at witnessing this sort of thing in the seemingly middle of absolutely nowhere. I treated myself to much introspection on these occasions and tucked away permanent memories of those moments of magic.

On other occasions, one's hold on human life seemed so very

fragile. Held high above this remote corner of the world, in a flying machine so tentatively suspended in three dimensions of space and one dimension of time, over areas of the Tibetan Himalayas so desolate that our maps in some areas were stamped "unexplored." What was one's state of mind? Did one sometimes feel disconnected from reality? Oh, yes!

It was in this context, on the disconsolate side of things, that I found one flight situation in particular more than a little depressing. It was those late afternoon flights over Tibet, transitioning from the incredible beauty of the play of sunlight on the snow covered mountain peaks, toward emerging dusk. Flying east, away from the disappearing setting sun, the sky would first turn a deep, depressing purple-gray, then gray-black and then a feeling of nothingness as we approached the blackness of China. And it was so cold. Cold. Cold! Condensation from my oxygen mask freezing on my fur collar.

For me, the isolation, the sense of endless void, particularly when one was living on the edge of fatigue from too many tightly scheduled Hump crossings, was sometimes difficult to deal with... even though I considered myself an upbeat person. While my subconscious never lost the ever presence of God, fatigue from time to time, flying under such conditions, caused me to succumb, temporarily at least, to one's mortality.

In any case, twilight now gone, blackness of night in hand, putting my head on straight with apology to my guardian angel for my too-human lapse in pondering my mortality, I turned to my very good friend—the instrument panel—and got down to the business of the descent into China and the approach to Chengtu... looking forward to some time around the pot-belly stove in the mess tent and a hot cup of coffee.

Speaking of guardian angels, their messages often come quite indirectly. Of many instances, here is only one example: On takeoff out of China for the return trip to Jorhat, our nose wheel tire had blown out and I did not know it. It must have happened at a point in takeoff where the nose wheel loading had lightened just before leaving the ground. Now, when a cargo B-24 lands empty, it has a far-forward center of gravity and on landing it tends to pitch onto the nose wheel at high speed. On the night approach to Jorhat, my copilot asked if I would demonstrate a landing with landing lights "off."

This kind of approach involves "feeling" for the runway with low power and the nose held high. In this case, after touchdown, I held the nose up as long as possible just for fun. At very low speed I let the nose wheel down and we came to a slowed stop on the blown out nose wheel tire. Had the normal landing procedure been used, the blown tire on high-speed impact would have torn off the B-24's marginally designed nose gear which, as previous accidents attested, would have had very serious consequences. Yes, one's guardian angel often applies indirect methods to resolve certain situations. Was this just an odd coincidence?... I don't think so.

Of the many varied experiences and scares in Hump flying, my first direct brush with the enemy was a most interesting one.

One afternoon, on the southerly route to Kunming, flying in the clear, one of the sharpest wrenches to my gut in all of my flying occurred. A stark, rising sun Japanese Zero pulled up in formation just outside my window. What to do? Nothing! We just sat there in our lumbering, sitting duck transport with no armament and no cloud cover to duck into. Then, what happened? An unexpected and most welcome surprise, the pilot of the Zero glared at us and simply flew away. I couldn't believe it. Why didn't he shoot us down? A bit of enemy compassion for a sitting duck? Or what?

The infamous Tokyo Rose of World War II offered the answer in one of her moral-dampening radio broadcasts. She said in perfect English that there was little to be gained in shooting down our hump-flying aircraft because we were littering the mountains with crashes all by ourselves. She said the Japanese aircraft would be saving their ammunition for more effective applications. Sadly, a book entitled "The Aluminum Trail"—an accounting of hundreds of lost hump aircraft scattered across the Himalayas—supported Tokyo Rose's ugly thought.

While some of our aircraft may have been shot down in flight, I must say I have no direct knowledge of this. Indeed, our air bases were bombed and strafed often enough to support Tokyo Rose's contention. The kind of scare we had on that flight never happened to me again, but left a lasting impression.

While other kinds of scary incidents will be covered in the course of this chapter, I should note that during the entire Hump flying experience and its many life threatening situations, my deep religious convictions entered in quite fervently… but not in an easily articulated context.

In the light of a constant self-imposed demand for greater spiritual growth on my own part, it was soon found that responding to religious conviction while involved in demanding secular environments had many shadings and nuances. This even appeared to some observers as if I was insensitive to God and prayer. An illustration of my so-called insensitivity is offered in order to rationalize, at least in part, my point of view on the subject.

We were flying at night into the worst of a violent thunderstorm, fast accumulating an ungainly load of ice and being tossed about the sky like a cork, with blinding lightning flashes and static electricity clawing at the canopy. My first time copilot, getting his first Hump indoctrination flight, got out of his seat, dropped to his knees behind the seat and while grasping the cockpit floor fitting to steady himself, bowed his head in a loud wailing prayer.

I can still see his terror-stricken face as I grabbed him by the scruff of the neck and shouted, "Get your ass back in your seat! We'll pray later!" I had my own fears to deal with and his method was definitely not the way!

In any case, that pilot got the word around to some extent and for a while I was thought of by some pilots as religiously insensitive. My own approach was one of entering into a few moments of quiet, private prayer before a flight and then letting God and his angels guide my in-flight actions. However, this *never*, even for a moment, meant setting aside a very aggressive bending of all my training, experience and human faculties to the flight task at hand... "The Lord helps those who help themselves."

Parenthetically, I was a long time gaining a partial understanding of why so many pilots of deep religious conviction were killed in the line of flight duty. Perhaps insufficient attention to the above admonition? I'm not sure.

Actually, at the time of the above described incident, I had just been asked by my protestant church to become a card carrying wartime minister, based on earlier special church training. That appointment was declined, however, because for some reason I did not understand at the time, the appointment didn't seem right for me. While I did not always heed the Biblical admonition—"God leadeth thee in paths thou knowest not of"—my intuition in this case said to wait. The reason for declining that appointment became clear only a few days later.

While relaxing on the porch of my basha, somewhat pooped form too many tightly scheduled Hump crossings, writing a letter to my dear wife, who I missed so very much, the base commander's executive officer approached. He said Colonel Barksdale wanted to see me in his office. Now, what was this all about? He had already awarded me the Air Medal and the Distinguished Flying Cross for some eighty Hump crossings up to that time and, all in all, things were going as well as could be expected.

As I entered his office, he greeted me warmly, offered me a cup of coffee and we chatted a bit on things in general. I should note at this point that Col. Barksdale was much respected by us all. While he was a rigorously tough-minded West Point military man, he was, more importantly, a fair and kind man—a gracious man. The man facing him, a maverick civilian in military uniform, respected him enormously. Moreover, he had flown the Hump many times and understood its problems.

He then got down to business and pointed out that the current chief pilot had completed his tour of duty and was going home. He said he was aware of the official commendation I had received for my work as head of the twin engine transition school at Long Beach, and with eighty Hump crossings under my belt involving almost every conceivable condition, he felt I had been sufficiently hardened to take on the appointment as Chief Pilot. My initial emphasis, he directed, since the chief pilot was also the Director of Training, was to address the acute shortage of aircraft commanders we were faced with... I gulped and thanked him for his confidence in me.

This appointment, much to my surprise, also included a host of peripheral duties in addition to Director of Training. Included were sub-positions as head of the Accident Investigation Board, member of the Operational Systems Planning Group and President of the Jungle Recreation Camp. Even the jungle camp involved a host of overseeing duties ranging from maintaining our jungle landing strip at the base of the mountains to the care and feeding of two hunting elephants. All this, together with maintaining my own flying schedule, made for quite a full life.

Now that I knew what I was to do in my unexpected assignment as chief pilot, it seemed appropriate to explain my reason for declining the appointment as a wartime minister. In a letter to church officials it was explained that I did not feel that capacity could be served by me and at the same time properly exhibit the flight discipline and oftentimes fair-minded firmness required to direct the activities of several hundred pilots and air crewmen of many religious persuasions—not to mention the nonbelievers. Instead, it was indicated I would work privately through the base chaplain on certain problems which, because of my position as chief pilot, there was more direct access to pilots' emotional problems than available to him. In any case, I often found myself acting as an ad hoc minister anyway on those occasions when pilots brought their problems directly to me. We simply shared. Their concerns were my concerns.

I did some heavy praying on all of the above, seeking God's guidance in executing that which, for me, was an enormous task. The assignment as chief pilot of the world's toughest possible airline operation struck me as an awesome task for a man of twenty-six—particularly with too many flight crews getting killed in the course of their efforts to reckon with the Himalayan Beast. It was certainly the last position I would have sought for myself. But at the same time, I had a deep down feeling I was put there for a reason. And I did have some ideas on how to reduce the number of lives we were losing. Heretofore, I had no official voice and could only discuss these ideas informally with pilot friends.

To begin with, the outgoing chief pilot introduced me to my office staff comprised of two clerks, Sergeant Sherry and Sergeant Miller. Sgt. Miller was the flight crew scheduler, a vital position, working with the chief pilot on crew composition in order to balance personalities and strengths. There was also Steve Lesseur, a competent ex-business man who kept the administrative paper flow in good order, including the logistics of the jungle recreation camp. I added one staff member, Lt. Bill Pike, a flying officer who had worked with me at Long Beach in a special restructuring of pilot background files—a non-alphabetical file based on pilot backgrounds, ratings and attitudes.

I was also assigned a personal jeep as well as a "flying jeep" in the form of an open cockpit, low wing trainer. The flying jeep was used for buzzing up the Subansiri River to the jungle camp on overseeing duties. A C-47 (DC-3) was also assigned for transporting people to and from the jungle camp and for occasional trips to Calcutta. Indeed, I was off to a good start with an excellent office staff and assistant check pilots: Stuart Childs, Jim Dewey, Court Remele, George Marville, Vardy Ramseur and others.

At the time of my appointment as chief pilot, pilot shortage had become so acute that we were into double trips. That is, as a crew completed deliveries of supplies over the Hump and returned empty, they were sent out again for another round trip just as soon as their airplane was reloaded. This was inherently a dangerous practice. I had performed a number of double trips, and on that fourth crossing to home base, staying awake was extremely difficult, no matter how many cups of bad coffee one consumed, not to mention the added risk of possibly impaired judgement.

On this matter of impaired judgement, I must confess to a mistake of my own which nearly proved fatal. It happened on my fourth consecutive Hump crossing without rest. We were on the ground at Chengtu, sitting in the aircraft waiting for the control tower to call us to the effect that light snow flurries had lifted enough to see down the runway for an instrument departure. In about half an hour, the tower called us to start engines and report to the south end of the runway for a takeoff to the north.

Now, with rare exception, we are normally cleared to the north end of the runway for a takeoff to the south. Usually, the last words from the tower were, "You are cleared for takeoff. After takeoff make an immediate *left* turn to avoid mountains to the west." This time, however, the tower said, "You are cleared for takeoff. After takeoff make an immediate *right* turn to avoid mountains to the west."

In my tired, judgement-impaired state of mind, we took off. I reacted to habit and instead of responding to the instruction to turn right, I turned left *toward* the mountain. We had reduced power to climbing mode and I was already into 90 degrees of the turn when my guardian angel smacked me unceremoniously across the head and said, "You turned left instead of right! No, it's too late to make an 'S' turn back to the right. You don't have room for that. Your best bet is to stay in the turn you're already into, apply full power and rack up the airplane in as steep a bank as you dare and complete a reversal of direction." Obviously, we made it. Otherwise my odyssey on wings of discovery would have ended then and there. Needless to say, I was more than wide-awake for the rest of that night.

But that night was not through with me yet. On that fourth consecutive crossing, I encountered my first severe battle with fatigue-laden pilot vertigo. We were on instruments in rather smooth air. Suddenly, half of the airplane emerged into bright moonlight on the edge of a very flat, vertical cloud form. The illusion of being in a vertical bank to what appeared to be a horizontal cloud form was so intense that every physical sense screamed to roll out level. But one's mind had to yell still louder, ignoring physical sensation and stay with what the instrument panel was saying to the mind. Yielding to the illusion of vertigo can all too easily result in loss of control. A real battle with my fatigued self—a kind of battle I had never before experienced—went on for an interminable thirty or forty seconds. The mind finally won the argument. The physical senses came into alignment with the mind and we proceeded on.

Under the heading of pilot fatigue, a heartbreaking tragedy that, sadly, happened more than once was this: We were on a return trip in very calm air shortly after dawn. We had just started our letdown into the valley and home base. We looked out ahead and in the far, far distance saw one of our airplanes that had not started its letdown into the valley. Heartbreaking, indeed! The crew was obviously asleep. Though our aircraft did not have auto pilots, a sleeping pilot, with his hands loosely on the control wheel, could be sound asleep in a properly trimmed airplane in calm air and could fly on until fuel supply was exhausted. Without success we tried to raise him on the radio and also asked the more powerful Jorhat base radio to try to raise him. No response. No way could we overtake the airplane and bump its wing tip—even at full power, since we were given only enough fuel to return to base with virtually no fuel reserve. Hence, that distant airplane overflew the Assam Valley and disappeared into the wildest reaches of the Himalayas and was never heard from again.

Another and hard to believe sleeping pilot situation was this: A sleeping pilot, whose aircraft had let itself down to an altitude below cruising altitude, was rudely awakened with a scraping sound. Now, one does not run into a mountain and fly away! But this pilot did exactly that! The configuration of the B-24 is such that its deep fuselage hangs below the propeller tips. He literally scraped the top of the mountain, pulled up smartly with full power and returned to cruising altitude. I could hardly believe his story until, on inspecting his airplane, found the bottom of the fuselage had been gutted like a fish. How very fortunate that crew was. Only one foot lower and they would never have left that mountain!

Indeed, we simply had to resolve this problem of no breaks

between Hump missions. Once over and return was more than enough without a rest period. Shortage of airplane commanders was number on priority to be addressed by the chief pilot's office.

Working first with Lt. Pike on pilot records, we reconstituted all of the files on our pilots' backgrounds. We broke the files down by pilots and copilots who had B-24 flying hours and a separate file for B-17 pilots and copilots. The point of this breakdown was that the B-17 was a very easy airplane to fly and very forgiving of pilot mistakes. The B-24, on the other hand, was more difficult to fly and less forgiving of pilot mistakes. While the cockpit procedures for these two four-engine aircraft were similar, our most immediate resource for new airplane commanders was to be found in those pilots and copilots who had B-24 background. We went to work on this point and found the approach to additional airplane commanders a valid one since it was the first step toward eliminating the random approach to utilization of our pilot resources.

We also scrutinized all pilot backgrounds for not only flying hours by type of aircraft, but by the grades they were given in the course of their flying careers. All airplane commanders were also put on alert to advise the chief pilot's office of those stronger copilots who showed above average potential. In this context, we remained alert to not overlook some copilots who might have less experience but evidenced a strong sense of the degree of aggressiveness required to assume command. That is, some good pilots would forever remain good copilots on the Hump operation because of insufficient "take charge" psyches.

We were gaining rapidly on overcoming our airplane commander shortage and simultaneously pushing for transfer of additional copilots to our Jorhat base.

As it was, we had a number of equally important issues to resolve, and they had to be tackled simultaneously. The number one issue after pilot shortage which could be dealt with immediately was the surprising number of pilots lost on night takeoffs.

On night takeoff, crashing into the jungle shortly after leaving the end of the runway, almost never happened on daylight takeoffs…

Why? To begin with, on a night takeoff, all outside reference to the ground completely disappeared on leaving the end of the runway. Control of the aircraft, while only a few feet above the surface, was wholly dependent on instruments.

In the process of discovering why we were experiencing these losses, it turned out to be the incorrect takeoff procedure called for in the B-24 operations manual. The coffee-sipping guy who wrote the manual, probably in the cozy confines of some engineering office, simply had no understanding of either the often unique operational situation involving a heavy overload, or no understanding of the aerodynamics related to that situation.

The operations manual incorrectly directed that the nose wheel be lifted as soon as possible after applying full takeoff power. The problem was that the airplane not only immediately took on additional aerodynamic drag on the takeoff run, but flew off the end of the runway at a wing angle to the airstream greater than the optimum wing angle for an overloaded condition. On a daylight takeoff, this was still not efficient, but not critical because the pilot could *see* the jungle and simply flew at a less efficient wing angle while the landing gear was retracting and until a stable climbing speed was achieved.

At night, however, wholly dependent on the instrument panel, some pilots, right after leaving the end of the runway, would try to level off a bit until optimum climbing speed was achieved. There was a terrible price paid for this. Leveling off a bit was not at first an increase in speed, but instead there was a brief settling of the aircraft as it sought to adjust itself to the proper climbing attitude. Only a few feet off the ground at night, the pilot was not immediately aware of this brief settling. Tragically, the overloaded airplane settled into the jungle in a massive ball of flame.

In my new, unasked for position as chief pilot, I mandated my own takeoff procedure, B-24 Operations Manual notwithstanding. The newly mandated procedure was to apply full takeoff power with hands loosely on the control wheel. Back pressure on the wheel to raise the nose wheel was to be applied gently only upon reaching the 100 mph mark. By that time, the end of the runway was approaching and a small additional increase in back pressure on the wheel lifted the overloaded aircraft off the runway at an optimum speed and climbing angle... Night takeoff crashes ceased immediately!

The next issue to be tackled was the number of aircraft fouling up their navigation by trying to dodge weather ahead. On a moonless night, it simply didn't matter since one could not see the weather ahead and flew through it *on course* anyway. That was it. Hold the required compass course, no matter what. We could not teach pilots the impossible task of dodging weather, but we could teach them to hold the airplane right side up while holding compass course through bad weather. That was the next mandate, to not only hold course, but to not climb or descend in an attempt to shake a load of ice. Carry the ice up the limits of engine temperature at increased power, or dump cargo. But hold compass course and altitude.

At this point, I should put a modest qualifier on the policy and procedural changes I was initiating. I was praying a great deal daily in asking God for His guidance; and then letting my maverickness proceed briskly in mandating whatever changes I thought necessary— time being of the essence in an effort to get the job done with a minimum of lost life... My deeply held belief is that "God perfecteth that which concerneth me." Not me doing it, but God through me as His servant. Of course, I'm the first to admit that I expect to spend a lifetime learning to practice this belief with consistency.

In this general context, I should also note that at this most critical period in my life so far, I found my stated of mind to be one of overwhelming love for my fellow man. The comradery among us as we strove against a common enemy in our effort to stay alive was a great feeling. And here I was, appointed to an enormous task, but with a tremendous opportunity to honor God in my efforts to add some comfort and reassurance to my fellow man. This was a heartwarming experience I shall never forget.

Now to deal with too many flights being directed over the far northern route to Chengtu regardless of prevailing weather—together with the stiff price of too many lost aircraft and crews. I immediately directed that all Chengtu flights be routed on the middle route unless acceptable weather permitted reasonably safe use of the northern route. The middle route policy meant turning north only after clearing the lower mountain peaks of the middle route with its more accessible emergency landing fields should trouble arise... which it did all too often!

However, a problem arose from this new policy. Our Hump base, together with other Hump bases, was required to submit monthly reports to Division Headquarters in Calcutta on tonnage of cargo delivered per flying hour. Since my advocacy required an extra forty minutes flying time to Chengtu, tonnage per flying hour from our Jorhat base was a little on the low side. But! The reduction in lost aircraft was dramatic.

Col. Barksdale called me into his office for a discussion of this. Agreeing with me, of course, on the reduction of losses, he pointed out that headquarters was criticizing him for our flying hours versus tonnage delivered. Obviously, I was distressed over having to abandon a policy that had clearly proven to be a life saving policy. Bless his fair-minded heart, the Colonel made a deal with me. While I had flown the far northern route many times—which was the very reason for my middle route policy—he directed that I fly the northern route exclusively for one month. Then, if I continued to feel strongly about that issue, he would support my middle route policy.

So, every other night I closed my office and flew the northern route exclusively for one month. It continued to be as bad as I had previously experienced; inordinately vicious weather, wing ice loads requiring a dash for the lower southerly routes and alternate landing bases, sometimes having to dump cargo, and, almost as dreaded as running out of fuel, an oxygen system leak warning light, forcing us to scramble for breathable air at a lower altitude and, finally, occasional engine failures and related problems. I was more convinced than ever. Col. Barksdale allowed me to continue with the middle route policy, except for acceptable weather on the far northern route.

However, running the chief pilot's office and flying the northern route every other night was taking its toll on me physically. While my nerves and emotional state remained in good shape, I was simultaneously brought down by throat-draining rear sinuses, diarrhea and eyes so glued shut with foreign mucous upon awakening in the morning that it required several minutes to bathe them open. The base doctor grounded me for a while. But at least I could run the office and work on other problems.

In a couple of weeks, the doctor put me back on flying status and I decided to take my first semi-rest break. By semi-rest, I refer to a low altitude flight to one of the Air Force aircraft overhaul stations on the southernmost tip of India, near the city of Bangladore. Another freshly overhauled airplane due to be returned to Jorhat wouldn't be ready for a few days. At a 3,000 foot altitude, Bangladore was somewhat cooler and a nice place to visit.

While we were there, the operations officer, an old friend from Long Beach, said he was short of pilots that week and asked if I would like to fly the weekly logistics run to Bombay in their C-47. This would be an overnight stay returning the next day. Another interesting break, having always wanted to visit Bombay. The Bangladore crew assigned to accompany me had other plans. So, after visiting the city for the afternoon, I returned to the base and was taken to the officer's quarters and club. The Air Force club was something else. They had taken over a palatial residence overlooking the Arabian Sea. I was assigned a private room with a large tile bath and a balcony overlooking the sea. It had been a long, long time since I had slept in a real bed instead of a narrow bunk. Big deal! Dinner in the massive dining room with only a dozen or so resident officers was also quite an experience—white tablecloths, fancy dinnerware and good food. Those guys lived really well.

Returning to Bangladore the next day, in May 1945, we were greeted by the wonderful news that found everyone rejoicing—VE Day! World War II was on its way toward final closure.

Our overhauled airplane was ready and we had a nice, low altitude return trip to our jungle base at Jorhat...Back to business, but greeted with the very sad news that we had lost another aircraft and crew for reasons unknown. This kind of news was always particularly difficult to digest for me. As chief pilot, I felt a sort of undefinable responsibility for that sort of thing. In discussing this with Col. Barksdale, he said, "Don't go there in your thinking." He pointed out that he wrestled with similar feelings every time he was faced with the lonesome task of writing letters to the surviving families... not easy.

We were now well into developing additional airplane commanders, having moved through the B-24 pilot file and into the B-17 file and beyond. On the early flights of new airplane commanders, we drew from out twin-engine pilot file the copilots with stronger backgrounds in order to reinforce the level of cockpit talent to the maximum possible. Joining me in this effort, Sgt. Bob Miller, our crew scheduler, was very sensitive and capable in matching crew capabilities and personalities in the cockpit. A real safety payoff here.

Along with our very competent instructor pilots, I was also giving indoctrination flights and checkout flights. On one particular flight, I was grateful to be giving an indoctrination flight to a very good friend, Courtney Remele, a strong pilot from Long Beach who was qualified for immediate assignment as airplane commander.

This particular flight was reasonably routine until we approached Jorhat on the return flight. Jorhat's weather had suddenly gone to zero-zero. We received notice a little too late to seek out an alternate landing base. As noted earlier, we were given only enough fuel to return to home base with virtually no reserve fuel. Fuel was the major commodity we delivered over the Hump, and the operations officers in China were very stingy with the amount of fuel to be given for return to India. It was not uncommon for returning airplanes to approach with a fuel-dry engine, which meant, of course, that the other three engines were close to running dry as well.

In this case, it was very fortunate that, in addition to our radio compass beacon, we had installed an ILS (Instrument Landing System) only two weeks earlier. It had been checked out but not yet used under actual blind landing conditions… until this dark night. Without enough fuel to apply full power and go around again in the event of a missed approach, it was a one shot deal, and all done from the cockpit. No comforting ground-based controller helping with a readable screen on the pilot's position. We didn't have that level of luxury. This was a first for me and a first for my friend, Remele.

Lining up on the ILS via our radio beacon initial approach, we were ready. Normally, I always handled my own throttles with my right hand on the four throttles and my left hand on the control wheel. This time I wanted both hands on the control wheel in order to better concentrate on the miserable little two-inch dial tacked on to the bottom of the instrument panel as an afterthought. This dial had two crosshairs. The vertical one was for runway alignment, the other for glide path. The name of the game was to keep the two crosshairs perfectly centered until the runway was reached. Remele would handle the throttles.

Now, when the ILS beam is first secured from the cockpit a couple of miles from the runway, the crosshairs are relatively easy to align. But as the beam narrows toward the runway, the slightest over-control can throw the crosshairs out of alignment. I asked Remele to sing out the moment he saw a runway light. We were at least blessed with smooth air. But the last few seconds of the flight became unexpectedly difficult. We were approximately a half-mile off the end of the runway at an altitude of less than two hundred feet when number one engine ran out of fuel, pulling us to the left of the runway. I knew beforehand this could happen, but it still took me by surprise. There was no going around again on a missed approach procedure. Nor was there time to play ILS crosshairs. I made an 'S' turn to the right and back to what I hoped was runway alignment.

Remele shouted, "I've got a light! Throttles closing."

For the first time I took my eyes off the instrument panel and initiated a backpressure on the wheel for the landing flare. We touched down hard on the extreme left side of the runway, barely missing the metal cones on top of which the runway border lights were mounted. We braked to a stop in the dense fog, steering by reference to the runway border lights outside my left window.

After a deep breath or two and a bit of brow mopping, Remele turned to me and said, "My God! Is this what Hump flying is all about!"

As opposed to the temporary gut wrench accompanying a sudden engine failure, an emergency approach to a one-shot blind landing does not evoke a gut wrench. One's though process is a quietly focused, deliberate piece of intense concentration. The vital point here is that not a single moment is wasted in thinking about the possibility of death that would ensue if the blind landing is not successfully executed. Absolute surety of proper execution of the approach is all that fills one's mind at the time. If success is to be the outcome, there is no room in the mind for any other thought.

All in all, things were settling down as much as could be expected under the circumstances. The most rewarding thought of all was that not only had we overcome our pilot shortage, but also the loss of aircraft and crews had dropped dramatically.

This brings me to one of my favorite episodes of flying the Hump. I might be accused of being a bit too smug in the story I'm about to relate, but so be it.

Col. Barksdale called me into his office one day to introduce his chief pilot to the Colonel who had just arrived in India. He was to be given his Hump indoctrination flight before taking over as commanding officer of another Hump base. I was elected to give him his indoctrination flight.

Well! Wha-da-ya know! It was Col. Snothead himself—the man who so ungraciously hired me, that green kid, as a civilian pilot. My, oh my. What a difference three years can make. Col. Snothead was to be my copilot. He said he remembered me, but I don't think he remembered his snotty, ungracious approach to hiring me... Oh, well. Here we go.

Our takeoff was early on a black night with a nearly full moon due later on. As we rolled down the runway in our overloaded beast, the colonel's first surprise was the amount of runway we were using to become airborne. His next surprise was the utter blackness as we left the end of the runway. Now stabilized in our climbing mode, he asked why we were flying west when the Hump was east. I explained we had to traverse the entire valley in order to clear the first ridge of the Hump on our climb out. This trip was to Kunming on the middle route and, under a rising moon, was quite beautiful. The trip was uneventful except for a relatively mild thunderstorm or two.

Cargo delivered and a bite to eat, it was time to file our return flight plan and to sign for our return fuel. The colonel immediately protested the amount of fuel. "Where's the reserve?" he asked. The Kunming operations officer explained the facts of life to him.

Our takeoff for return to Jorhat was in an empty airplane and we climbed briskly out over the moonlit lake to our cruising altitude. Shortly after reaching that altitude, we entered into full instrument flight in the usual unknown solid overcast. It was extremely turbulent with the expected lightning flashes and dramatic clawing of static electricity around the cockpit canopy.

Then, Whamo!... We hit the severest vertical wind sheer that I had encountered in more than one hundred thirty Hump crossings. The first thing that happened as we entered the vertical wind sheer was a radical drop in airspeed. Forward airspeed dropped to below stalling speed and kept on dropping. I pushed the control wheel forward and, again to my surprise, the wheel traveled all the way forward with virtually no resistance to the sharply reduced horizontal airstream. When the forward wheel movement to down-elevator finally took hold, we were in a near vertical dive and still going up with power off!

"My God," I said to myself. "The Really Big One has finally knocked on my cockpit door."

I eased into a level flight attitude, power off and still rising. We were now integrated with that super-strong vertical rising air mass. Accompanying turbulence was so severe that it was difficult maintaining sensory identification with the instrument panel. At one point, the turbulence threw us into a near ninety-degree bank. I thought that for a few seconds we were going to be flipped on our back. Full right wheel and hard right rudder and we seemed to hang interminably on our side before returning to a level flight attitude. We were then spit out the top of the thunderhead at over forty thousand feet in bright, most welcome moonlight.

I applied power again, as the aircraft seemed to shudder in relief, along with its pilot, of course, that we were once again in control. We had now passed through that ridge of thunderstorms and we descended in the clear to cruising altitude. At that point, I had an exchange of glances with Col. Snothead. I can still see his saucer-sized eyes bugging out over his oxygen mask. Now in the clear and a moonlit trip for the rest of the way back to Jorhat, I treated myself to a deep chuckle. Smug of me, I know. But Col. Snothead owed me one. Over a cup of coffee after the flight, the colonel asked me if Hump flying was generally that bad. I simply said, "It happens, Colonel. It happens." Not very kind of me. But I was not inclined to tell him that his indoctrination flight was through the worst weather situation I had ever encountered.

In serious retrospect on the flight, not only had we hit the Really Big One we all waited for, but also it occurred to me that we were extremely fortunate to be flying an empty airplane with its inherently greater responsiveness to the flight controls. I had grave doubts about successfully dealing with that situation with a full cargo overload. Some of the aircraft we lost must have encountered the Really Big One with cargo overloads and were, sadly, unable to deal with its severity.

Interesting breathers from the rigors of Hump flying were not only first run movies that were sent to us, but, from time to time, top celebrities from the entertainment world visited our remote spot of the world. For me, the most memorable visit was by the famous orchestra leader, Andre Kostelanetz and his equally famous opera star wife, Lily Pons. He brought with him a staff of only two assistants, no orchestra. He spent a few days on our base, rounding up all of our amateur musicians with their respective tired string instruments and bent horns and actually assembled a nearly full orchestra from the hidden resources on our base.

On opening night in our outdoor theater, the Mosquitodrome, the respect for this great professional musician by our amateur musicians was so great that they not only performed magnificently, but the sound of that ad hoc orchestra, for most of us, compared quite acceptably with his formal orchestra. This was exceeded only by the magnificent voice of Lily Pons, carried out over the jungle night. Even the hyenas on the jungle perimeter were not laughing that night... A most thrilling experience.

So, back to the routine of indoctrination flights and checking out new airplane commanders. I encountered all types of pilots.

If Lt. Will Andrus reads this book, he will recall the following. He was, in my opinion, a very strong potential airplane commander who wanted to remain on copilot status. Unlike certain pilots who would, for sure, remain good copilots, Andrus had flown with me several times and in my judgement had the ability to assume command. He had a good sense of humor too—an important aspect of emotional stability.

One tired dawn, we took off from Chengtu on our return flight. I had forgotten to hook up my twelve-inch oxygen mask trunk to the aircraft's main oxygen supply. Andrus knew this, and when he thought I would soon be encountering anoxia—a very subtle, judgement - eroding oxygen starvation condition—he reached over, tipped up the trunk of my oxygen mask and dramatically dropped a peanut in it. I guess I was on the edge of anoxia, as this little bit of humor produced near hysterical laughter.

Upon our return, sharing a cup of coffee, I pointed out he was ready for his final check ride as airplane commander. He sadly complained he would not get out alive if he were put in the command role. I bet him ten bucks he would get out alive and said that since we were always on the edge of a shortage of airplane commanders, he was needed... I was away from the base when he completed his tour of duty and didn't get a chance to say goodbye. On my desk, with an appreciative note, was a crisp ten-dollar bill.

Another strong, rather crusty pilot, Lt. Pat Patterson, a true Texas cowboy who once rode a water buffalo into the officers' club while slightly under the influence, copiloted me on his Hump indoctrination flight. A small incident took place on takeoff. Occasionally, the turbo-supercharged B-24, when taking off with an ill-tuned, overly rich fuel mixture on one of the engines, would throw a dramatic torch of flame out the exhaust. Some flight engineers theorized, incorrectly, that this could burn one of the two vertical rudders aligned directly behind engines two and three. On our night takeoff, a new flight engineer, one who had not flown with me before, noted during the most critical part of the takeoff that we had a long flaming plume off number two engine.

The flight engineer shook my shoulder, "Number two torching, Captain." I was somewhat busy at the time, to say the least, so Patterson gently pulled him away from my ear and shouted in his ear, "Let the son-of-a-bitch torch!' Reducing power would always eliminate torching, but under these circumstances would also eliminate us. Torching was always allowed until the first power reduction for climbing mode was established. Under reduced power, the torching stopped immediately. Patterson's indoctrination flight was a relatively moderate one with no other incidents.

Then, there were other kinds of pilots: Those who were in the hospital for legitimate nervous disorders and were anxious to return to their regular flying duties. Also, in only a few cases, there were those pilots who, after a Hump flight or two, refused to fly. In those few sad cases, they would grab a whisky bottle and roll into the gutter until dishonorably discharged from service.

Then, there was the one of a kind case: An ex-airline captain who, after a couple of flights, refused to fly the Hump, stating that he could apply all of his acquired skills and stand only a 50-50 chance of surviving. His legal contention was that the Air Force had hired him as a civilian pilot and that they were in violation of their contract with him by forcing on him an officer's commission hi did not want. Somehow he had lost the realization that he was an American citizen, that a war was going on, and that none of us were particularly thrilled with what we were called upon to do.

His court martial case was opened on our base to a packed house. The prosecution dramatically opened the case by demanding the death penalty. A gasp from the crowd. After that first day, his case was moved to division headquarters in Calcutta. I do not know what finally happened to him, but the rumor was that he had been given a light sentence and a dishonorable discharge. The speculation was that his case had been dramatized on our base in order to get the word around that his approach to the situation was not very wise.

Many other Hump flying experiences encountered by myself and others could be shared, but I believe the reader gets the picture. It was now time to face a particularly unhappy day for me.

Our much-respected Col. Barksdale was promoted to a higher position at division headquarters. Unhappily, after a very productive tenure as chief pilot, largely due to the great support from Col. Barksdale, the new base commander and I did not get along at all.

This new colonel was not, in my opinion, a reasonable man. Among other things, he immediately dumped our middle Hump route policy and reinstated the northern route, regardless of weather.

One late afternoon, we were sitting on the end of the runway ready for takeoff clearance. The control tower called and said, "You are cleared for takeoff on the northern route to Chengtu."

After one hundred fifty Hump crossings and a bit weary of it all, this maverick, often with a distorted sense of military protocol, simply said to the tower, "This is Captain Miner. I filed for the middle route to Chengtu. We've already lost one aircraft today on the northern route. I'm not flying unless cleared on the middle route!"

"Stand by," said the tower. It was full fifteen minutes before the tower called back and said, "You are cleared for takeoff on the middle route to Chengtu."

Fortunately, the new commanding officer didn't have the guts to challenge me on this. He could have really screwed me for that act of insubordination. So, for himself, he did the next best thing. As chief pilot, I was due to be recommended for my majority. Forget it.

He threw that out the window… and I always thought it would be worth a chuckle to be called Major Miner. It was a good thing I had never intended a future military career.

So, in a wire to my former commanding officer in Calcutta, and without giving any details, a transfer was requested. I strongly suspect Col. Barksdale knew the reasons for my request and he responded immediately. As a reward, one supposes, for my work with him as chief pilot of his former base, he had me transferred to Calcutta as a special missions VIP command pilot on the general's staff. Since the generals were quite fussy about who was in the cockpit of the airplane they were traveling in, I felt honored by this assignment.

Flying the luxurious new, four-engine C-54 transport was, indeed, a most welcome change form the war weary old dogs we were flying up north. This assignment involved interesting flights all over the China-Burma-India theatre with an occasional thirteen-hour nonstop flight to the Philippines.

On one of our return flights from the Philippines at night across the South China Sea, passing the Japanese held Hainan Island, we encountered anti-aircraft fire. With a bright moon and no cloud cover to duck into, we zigzagged until that disconcerting episode was behind us. While we were previously given a submarine rendezvous location in the event of trouble, this was of little comfort. Locating the submarine, even assuming a successful ditching, didn't seem too likely.

So, on with the flight across Viet Nam, Thailand, Burma, the Bay of Bengal and to our Calcutta base at Barakapore. One interesting aspect of the flight was the lack of advance weather information on the middle portion of the flight, and the total lack of radio navigational aids for that long flight. Without a formal navigator working the star fixes, it was all magnetic compass until over the Bay of Bengal, where the radio compass needle could confirm our position. If the compass needle wandered, the pilot could call for a bearing from the Calcutta ground station. On this particular flight we called for a ground bearing. We were about twenty miles north of course. Not too bad, considering several stretched of bad weather along that thirteen hour flight.

Then came that joyous day in August when VJ Day was declared. The war was over! However, the duties for the VIP pilot staff intensified in transporting those officers involved in mop up operations across the China-Burma-India theatre. Still, along with others who had fulfilled their tour of duty requirements, I put in for return home. While waiting in the long line, we continued to fly our VIP missions.

One unhappy day, while between flights, relaxing by the swimming pool at the British-American Officers' Club in Calcutta, a friend brought me news that another of our Jorhat crews had just been killed on the northern Hump route.

What was going on here? The war was over! There was no longer any need for the northern or middle Hump routes. All logistics could now be easily handled off southern bases in the Calcutta area. My maverick blood was boiling. I was really pissed off. Ignoring all military protocol, I rushed to division headquarters and, without waiting to be admitted, stormed into one of Col. Barksdale's staff meetings.

In protesting vigorously, I spelled out what had just happened up north and urged that northern Hump operations be shut down immediately. Though many of the officers in the meeting knew me form VIP flights, and even though Col. Barksdale and I had a fine rapport based on mutual respect, he was obliged—understandably, I must confess—to put on his military protocol hat and, for my gross insubordination, order me confined to quarters until further notice.

He phoned me the next day, and without giving me a reason for his chuckle, invited me to have lunch with him at the headquarters officers' club. We sat down and, still chuckling, he first said to me, "You were pretty salty in there yesterday, storming my staff meeting the way you did. I just had to come down on you." He then went on to say, "After you left yesterday, I got hold of General Tunner and together we went in to see General Wedemeyer. Essentially, in a much quieter manner," he smiled, "we made the some case you were making for closing the northern Hump operation."

This turned out to be one of the happiest days of my life. They immediately initiated shut down proceedings... May there always be a place for the maverick civilian in military uniform.

At this point, my turn to go home had finally arrived. Since everybody wanted to go home all at once, air travel was impossible. Hence, a tedious sixteen-thousand mile journey by rail and ship via Karachi, the Arabian sea, the Red Sea, the Suez Canal, the Mediterranean sea, the Atlantic, a tedious train ride across the U.S. to California and, finally, home at last.

However, the period of weeks for the trip was not wasted. In my journal, I posed a basic question to myself: What were the most significant lessons learned during the previous, very intense four years? And how might these lessons be applied to the return to civilian life?

In that period, it seemed a virtual lifetime had been lived in the acquisition of knowledge of myself, other people and the world in general... not to mention the variables in working with a myriad of diverse cultures and professional backgrounds. The largest lesson of all was *what I did not know...* and the steps I should take to rectify this.

Hence, I prescribed for myself and informal lifetime study program in a continuing effort to fill the voids.

But as subsequent chapters will disclose, the professional paths that opened up were often totally unexpected and not always wisely handled. Though often rewarding, much of it all offered harsh professional lessons until that point in this eighty-year odyssey was reached where greater balance was obtained.

But the first order of business on reaching home was to embrace my dear, forbearing wife and take a couple of month's vacation, with the idea of starting a family and initiating construction of our home.

Chapter Four
Returning from Air Force to Big Corporation
The Cream of Corporate Positions and Its Price

Upon returning from overseas, my wife and I took a wonderful two-month holiday, visiting many of our favorite places at Santa Barbara, Palm Springs and Big Bear Lake. During that time, we started a family and arranged for construction of our home in West Los Angeles.

Then it was time to return to my former design engineering position at North American Aviation. The management there was very considerate. Recognizing my four-year absence, they not only gave the promotion I would have received had I stayed with them, but they adjusted my salary to make up for the normal salary raises I would have received during that period. Not bad. I was most appreciative.

While at some point I would present to the management my journal notes on the war years and their translation into a proposed new operational forum for design auditing and management, I would for a time go with the flow in the present context of things. While the aircraft industry had indeed furnished some fine military airplanes which played the dominant role in winning the war, there still existed an underlying communications gap between the perspective of the military operational people and the perspective of the non-operational aeronautical design engineering people. The attending operational inefficiencies and wartime losses due to this situation should be reckoned with before moving too far into the then just emerging jet age. But since realizing that those who directed traditional aeronautical engineering practices would not be easily persuaded to a dramatic change in modus operandi, it was first appropriate to reestablish myself in the design engineering domain.

But at first, something bothered me. I found many former associates a bit standoffish. Not exactly unfriendly, but not given to the former easy repartee we previously enjoyed. I discussed this at lunch with my good friend, Tom Johnson, asking him to help me sort it out. Tom nailed it down quickly. He pointed out that I simply was not the same man who left the company four years ago... and it showed, he said. I had lived an intense and dangerous life all over the world, had received my fair share of medals and had returned to a quiet engineering room environment—an environment which, for them, had not changed at all during those four years. They were the same people. Apparently, I was not the same. Yet, I felt my friendly old self toward them, even most appreciative of the fine support they had given to those of us on the operational firing line.

Tom suggested I just give it a little time. He said most of the guys are a little shy around you, having an inkling of what you must have gone through—that which they missed during those intense war years. Tom was right. Since my approach to them was simply an unassuming, glad-to-be-back attitude, things quickly settled down to a generally happy state.

My good intention in returning to my design engineering position was, at first, to fully enjoy the freedom from danger and the intensity with which, for four straight years, I had diligently applied myself to the avoidance of unforgiving mistakes in my flying. From now on, it meant life would be happily confined to an occasional mistake in the design room. This simply meant sitting back and casually thinking about correction of the mistake—after first going for a cup of coffee, of course. Ah, this was the life!

But, no, it wasn't the life!... Simply bored out of my head in only a couple of months, I couldn't seem to come down from the intensity of the previous four war years. As was the case with most war returnees, this feeling was not a healthy one and had to be dealt with. Fortunately, in my own case, an incredibly, anything but boring career opportunity presented itself. North American Aviation had just completed flight testing on the prototype of their first commercial airplane for the private consumer. Wanting desperately to be a part of that new program, what could one lose by asking. As one of the company president's lowly design engineers, I presumptuously but very politely knocked on President Kindelberger's door and asked if there was a place for me in his new commercial airplane program.

His first reaction was polite, but uncertain. He said management was looking for someone who had a working relationship with his engineering department for on-going product development reasons; and who also had a background as a decorated Air Force officer for public relations reasons. He further added that he wanted an Air Force flyer who had substantial experience in North American's famous airplanes—the B-25 Mitchell Bomber and the P-51 Mustang.

Sheeesh, was he trying to discourage me with the scope of his requirements? With my heart in my mouth, knowing this opportunity was tailored for me, it was modestly asked if an Air Force captain who had been awarded the Distinguished Flying Cross, two Air Medals and two battle stars, as well as extensive flying experience in both of his famous airplanes, and over two previous years as an engineer with his firm would be sufficient background.

"Well," said he with a friendly smile toward the eager young guy confronting him, "your background looks like a good fit, but I was looking for someone a little older to head up our not yet formed Commercial Airplane Marketing and Product Development Division. But let's give you a try as a flying marketing representative and engineering liaison man. We'll place you with our new Corporate Public Relations and National Marketing Staff which has been set up to deal exclusively with the private consumer... and we'll see where you go from there."

Subsequently, it was my good fortune to be promoted to General Manager of that new division of the company. Though still at the relatively tender age of twenty-seven, the previous highly intense years in both operational flying and Air Force management assignments had given me a measure of self assurance I did not previously possess.

It can be said that if one must work for a big corporation, I had the richest cream of all positions. My division of the company was housed in a separate building and large hangar on the flight line next to the main factory with a staff of three other pilots, an office staff, an engineering liaison office, a product development test staff and a maintenance group. My personally assigned airplane, which was specially equipped to my own specifications for instrument flying, was parked on the flight line just outside my office.

Our marketing and promotional efforts involved not only local flight demonstrations to celebrities and professionals from all walks of life, but flights to our customer locations and private ranch airstrips all over California, Nevada and Arizona. These out of town flights were prompted largely by the need to visit those customers who were suffering delays on our promised delivery dates and needed periodic assurance that they had made good decisions in buying our airplane.

Parenthetically, among various development and production problems, we had one particularly serious problem with the new composite-material propeller we were using on our airplane. Most fortunately, this problem was solved before production airplanes were placed in the hands of the purchasers. Here is another instance of my guardian angel at work.

I had flown our public relations director to a Las Vegas marketing conference of our newly formed national dealer group. After the dinner meeting, the director advised me that he was due back in Los Angeles for a meeting the following morning. So, on a clear moonless night, we took off for home. The night flight at 13,000 feet over the mountain range and into the Los Angeles basin was uneventful except that I wasn't satisfied with the engine's power output. I suspected a carburetor problem.

The next morning I took out this same airplane with our chief mechanic as passenger to see if we could nail down the power output problem. The takeoff went smoothly out of the LA Airport into a quite brisk 25 mph wind off the ocean. Still at a low altitude, we were passing over rolling, brush covered sand dunes when, with absolutely no warning whatsoever, a whole foot of one propeller blade broke off of our new composite-material propeller. I felt the engine would shake out of its mounts before I could shut it down.

What to do?... The scan at work again. While in plain view, there was no way of reaching the nice flat beach against a 25 mph headwind. The rolling sand dunes were way too rough for a decent landing, even with the landing gear retracted... a few seconds of deliberation... yes, with a 25 mph tailwind, I'll do a 180 degree turn and land downwind on the main runway. Even at our low altitude, our downwind speed should enable us to reach the main runway before touch down. A hasty call to the control tower to stop the next takeoff... and after a very hot downwind landing, we rolled out with plenty of runway to spare. In this case, the flight situation called for breaking the into-the -wind landing rule, but with little thought required as to available downwind landing distance.

I later recalled that *less than one flying hour* prior to this catastrophic propeller failure, we were flying over high rugged mountains on a moonless night. In delaying that propeller failure with so little margin, my guardian angel was certainly hard at work that night!

In any event, in almost all cases, the customer endorsement of North American's fame and reputation never ceased to amaze me. The private consumer in those early post war years simply wanted to be a part of it all. It was right after the war and President Kindelberger brought his good friend, General Doolittle, to the flight line for a demonstration of his new airplane. It was a real privilege to meet the widely acknowledged greatest pilot of that earlier era in aviation history.

As we stepped up onto the wing, I slid open the cockpit canopy, motioned to the left seat and with a smile asked, "Care to drive, Sir?"

He laughed and said, "Thanks, but I'll just enjoy the ride." So, with the general in the right seat and President Kindelberger in the back seat, we took off for a pleasant cruise of the Los Angeles coastal area. After thanking me for the flight, having noted the miniature one-inch ribbon pin in my coat lapel—which signified the DFC—he asked where I had served. A concurring few words were exchanged and the two of them took off to meet other people. For me, a most memorable experience.

Many celebrities, doctors, corporate executives, ranchers and others visited our flight line for demonstration flights or purchases. These visits were further augmented by North American's newly recruited public relations director, a former Hollywood executive who, I do believe, knew just about every movie star and director in Hollywood. He produced a constant stream of Hollywood visitors. Many of them purchased airplanes or displayed continuing interest and, while waiting for deliveries of the production model, made many repeat visits calling for additional demonstration flights and generally enjoying the post war airport ambience. Great fun.

Of the many stars and character actors I had the pleasure of meeting, I should like to make an observation on the top movie stars, who are not generally appreciated in real life terms. Stars like Robert Montgomery, Clark Gable, Dick Powell, Robert Taylor and others had a *real* presence and sense of command. Famous movie director, Victor Flemming, who bought one of our airplanes and came out for many additional flight demonstrations, became a friend. It was Flemming who introduced me to Clark Gable, who was not only gracious, but simply reflected a sense of command. It was easy to appreciate his wartime performance in combat situations.

Similarly, Robert Montgomery, a movie star who distinguished himself as a Navy PT boat commander during the war, always asked on his visits to fly over the naval installations in the Los Angeles and San Diego harbors. He liked to pull up memories of the war years. It was easy to visualize this man at the helm of a Navy PT boat in a battle situation *for real*, and not just playing a part. It was indeed a revelation to have some direct exposure to a few of those people who, normally, we saw only on the big screen.

This new social exposure was enlarged for me in co-hosting with President Kindelberger in his home a wide range of top people from many professional avenues. Also, as his corporate pilot, I often flew him and his wife to their desert home in Palm Desert. I was now thrust into a casual first name relationship with him. With a smile he said, "My name is 'Dutch' when we're in the cockpit of your airplane, but it's 'Mr. K' in corporate staff meeting."

It was at this juncture that my naïve outlook on big corporation politics started to fester. The envy of certain other corporate executives toward me over that which obviously was the cream of corporate positions, coupled with their growing annoyance over my personal rapport with the president of the corporation, was becoming a bit much for some of the more political corporate animals.

On this other side of the coin, I was thrust into the bowels of big corporation politics. Some painful lessons were learned there since I found myself a long way short of being a fencing master in the reconciliation of disputes with management. Mistakenly, I thought one could call the shots on urgently needed changes in product and policy and simply get on with it—not unlike certain urgent military situations… Not so! It eventually became painfully clear to me that this was not the way in big corporation life.

But larger problems were looming. North American's early post war, first commercial airplane program, soon encountered a number of product development and engine problems during the production process which promised to push the widely promoted selling price over the moon. As it was, by this time a large number of production deliveries had been made to a wide spectrum of buyers. All of those airplane deliveries were quite late, well beyond the promised delivery dates. Moreover, all were sold at a substantial loss because of sales contracts written at an early and more optimistic time. Even worse, all of those airplanes were subject to factory recall to fix various problems at company expense.

Thus, within only a couple of years from the inception of the program, though basically a fine airplane, top management decided that their first commercial airplane program was a bust. They decided to sell the entire program, including inventory and tooling, to another company in another city and to take a tax write-off.

So, what does one do now? My initial thought did not pan out. Having had great rapport with President Kindelberger, since it was my privilege to have been his corporate pilot and co-host of an endless stream of celebrities he proudly brought to the flight line and to his home, it seemed not unreasonable to expect to be slated for some other executive position.

But as it turned out, there was little or no rapport on my part with several of the top management people. Now that my division of the company was being abolished, certain members of management couldn't wait to pull the welcome mat out from under me. I was no longer wanted for some other position. It was also surprising to my young and then politically naïve perspective that President Kindelberger did not intercede in my behalf. Although he did write me a fine letter of recommendation, he yielded to the corporate political situation. Indeed, a painful lesson in corporate politics.

So, the last flight in my no-longer-personal-airplane was made to my last previously scheduled out-of-town meeting on company business. In returning at night, flying west through the mountain pass out of Palm Springs, the whole panorama of greater Los Angeles yielded a sparkling array on a night made crystal clear by a storm that had just passed. The air was smooth, the engine purring in its cruise mode, a symphony playing on the overhead radio speaker in the cockpit and my thoughts began to level out. This kind of flying, for all of my sadness at the turn of events, rarely failed to instill a sense of peace... sometimes a fleeting peace, but usually enough to get a fresh toe hold on things.

As to some of the more useful views of my tenure with North American Aviation, these are covered in a later chapter in which discussion is offered on how to flunk "Corporate Obedience School." As a not yet reconciled maverick, it will also be made very clear, through some painful introspection, that my professional setback was nobody's fault but my own.

In any case, this seemed to be a time to regroup; to not even seek a position elsewhere at that particular time. Not only was there a need to back off from the previous, more intense years of my professional life, but I certainly needed to spend some quality time with my much neglected family. Moreover, with my self assurance somewhat bent out of shape, some very serious thought had to be given as to where the hell I was going with my life. We decided to sell our home in West Los Angeles, lease a cabin on Big Bear Lake and, with our year-old baby, take a one-year sabbatical.

During that time my wife and I built our own mountain cabin in the pines just a short walk from the mountain landing strip that had been flown to so many times. The mental therapy of that labor served me well, even though I missed my flying.

Then, one afternoon, out of the blue soared an old Stearman biplane, landing gently on the strip. Needing a break from my carpentry, it was only a short stroll down to say hello to the stranger. Well, surprise, surprise! He was no stranger, but an old friend from our India-China Hump days... and another temporarily lost soul. He couldn't settle down either. He was still single, had received a family inheritance, bought the airplane and decided he would spend a year or two flying to every little out of the way landing strip he could find all across the country... spending some time at any one place that struck his fancy.

After some happy visiting with my old friend, Hal Bolin, he caught me looking longingly at his airplane. Any pilot knows that look.

"Here," said Hal, "take my helmet and goggles and go give yourself and airing out. I'm going across the field to that motel and freshen up. I'll see you for dinner."

It felt good to open the throttle and breeze down the airstrip, out over the lake and up over the mountain range rising from the lake shore. Actually, it was on this flight that a pivotal insight revealed itself. Unexpectedly, a contrast was observed between my outlook on life in the Air Force and my outlook on life in the post war corporate world. The primary difference, at the very core of things, came almost as "a blinding glimpse of the obvious." It was simply a basic difference in premise—spiritual insight versus gross materialism.

During the constant danger of Hump flying and, as chief pilot, seeing to the needs of hundreds of other pilots and air crewmen in those critical circumstances, I experienced a strong leaning on God and things spiritual. This, in turn, yielded an overwhelming sense of love and comradery toward all men in the common task we shared—getting the job done against a common enemy and trying to stay alive.

The post war corporate life, on the other hand, held no life and death stimulus toward things spiritual. While the spiritual side of life was not completely ignored, there was most certainly a drifting away from the diligence previously applied to it. I had simply succumbed to the glitz and glamour of movie stars and wealthy people and dealt with the secular world in what seemed to be a somewhat productive, but rather shallow, materialistic way.

That was it! The need for transcendence of the spiritual over the materialistic—practiced with more diligence, never perfectly in the secular world, but with a striving for enough consistency to make a difference. While future trying circumstances would occasionally cause me to drift from that noble thought, the present situation was going to be moved on track.

Reducing power, soaring around a golden-hued mountain peak at near sunset and down into the lake valley and the airstrip, much needed refocusing took place. The wheels gently crunched the airstrip and I taxied up to the sheltering pine trees and shut down the engine. As the propeller cranked down to its rest position, the not unpleasant mechanical smell of the airplane yielded to the sweet pungency of the forest. As the last rays of the setting sun shimmered on the lake and filtered through the trees, a gentle stillness pervaded my being, offering a fresh view of the totality of things.

Now ready to get my act together, the remaining time in the mountains would be invested in determining the next course of action in the most productive way. The question as to the most productive way, however, first required an answer to a much larger question: How had my overall design engineering viewpoint been shaped by intense wartime operational flying?

First, after once again acknowledging the good airplanes that won the war, the problem would be addressed through analyzing flight losses, accidents and failed missions that need not have occurred except for aircraft design features and pilot and crew accommodation factors which did not reflect the realities of military operational flying.

Unbelievably, the aerospace industry had no formal design management function chartered to monitor the ultimate operational purpose of their aircraft designs *during the design process.* In turn, they had no procedure for predetermining, at design board level, many of those operational conditions that the aircraft and its crew would eventually encounter. Sadly, operational flight analysis at design board level—not just *flight* analysis, but *operational flight* analysis—was not the conventional engineering wisdom. Monumental losses of aircraft and crews attributable to that situation, and the aerospace industry's unawareness of the significance of formalizing corrective design engineering practices, were to be addressed.

The response to that situation is offered in summary for now, since variations on that theme appear in subsequent chapters. A basic write up was composed which was based on establishing a top ranking staff reporting to the chief engineer, with an unrestrained liaison member of the staff reporting directly to top corporate management.

This staff would be comprised of a blend of engineering graduates who were also ex-Air Force or ex-Navy pilots; ex-Air force Aero Medical Laboratory engineers and scientists; ex-military operational planners and logistics experts; ex-Department of Defense air technical intelligence experts; and one of the corporation's test pilots.

The basic function of this group would be to model the structure of the entire operational mission with *all* of the *external* operational mission factors bearing on the aircraft; charted from the end point of the mission and working rearward into the actual design of the aircraft.

Operational mission model delineated, the above defined Operational Flight Analysis Staff would then evaluate, audit and reconcile intra-engineering department disputes at design board level... and believe it, there are disputes. In this regard, the aerodynamics department, which dominates the aircraft design scene, is the most difficult to deal with in reckoning with their inordinate proclivity for speed and maneuverability—often at the expense of more vital operational considerations such as pilot and crew accommodation, the environment in which the operational flight would take place and so forth. This traditional engineering conventional wisdom has often inhibited good design.

In short, the new management objective in aircraft design would be based on considering the whole of things *before* the operational fact. The appalling lack of dedicated *interdisciplinary coordination* across the various military and industrial specifications involved will be shared in following chapters as one of the underlying, more significant aspects of this odyssey.

To draw on an old adage, notwithstanding the degree to which, even today, it receives only lip service: *"The whole is greater than the sum of the parts."*

In any case, plans were laid out to approach some of the larger aerospace firms with the scope and potential of the concept. It was also my firm decision that, however it might all turn out, the central thrust of my professional life had been found—shaped by the metaphors of flight... in short, *wholeness of purpose and concept* delineated at the outset of any system design effort.

But first, it was necessary to move down from the mountains and establish a new home, particularly now that we were running out of money. We had just enough left for a down payment on a small home and to search for a job.

Chapter Five
A Tortuous Path Back to the Air Force
Seeking a Forum for a New Philosophy of Design

In seeking a new position, since we were now seriously low on funds, it was necessary to hold pride of position in abeyance and to proceed as quickly as possible to acquire a design engineering position in the context of the conventional wisdom. Presentation of my Operational-Flight-Analysis engineering management concept would have to be approached at some near future time. We simply could not afford the time it would probably take to find an appropriate executive position in some new company.

Since a position at any level in my former company was not a viable option, I arbitrarily picked the Lockheed Aircraft Corporation. I applied for a design engineering position, and, if possible, working in whatever department was handling cockpit and flight station design. That position was acquired and I immediately found myself lost in a sea of design boards in Lockheed's vast engineering division.

I did as I was told by a friendly supervisor for a couple of months and then decided to sound him out on approaching engineering management on my proposed engineering management concept. Intelligent and gracious though he was, it was like hitting a brick wall. He said that approaching management with such an idea was unthinkable. I wouldn't think of trying to go around him, so I worked there another month or two while seeking a job with some other aircraft company.

This turned out to be Northrop Aircraft Corporation. They had just received an Air Force contract to go ahead with the development of their massive, eight-engine flying wing bomber. They were hiring design engineers at better salaries and I secured a position in their cockpit and flight station design section. The flight station design task was a comprehensive one, involving the cockpit proper for pilot and copilot and a separate station for the flight engineer with duplicate controls for eight engine throttles, fuel management distribution valves, related instruments, and so forth.

A word on the flying wing: Long a dream of its designer and company founder, Jack Northrop, the massive wing in flight was truly a beautiful sight to see. However, the flying wing was a "calm air concept" in which operational consideration of its behavior in turbulent air had not been considered—unimaginable as that might sound. The wing had almost no sweepback for longitudinal stability and control—the kind of longitudinal stability found in *all* other types of airplanes. Notwithstanding the vast improvement in aircraft design over the years, the same principle of longitudinal stability has obtained almost as far back as the Wright brothers. It's the simplest of aerodynamic concepts—airflow control "leverage" from a tail section located well behind the airplane's center of gravity. Mandatory for control in turbulent air.

My access to top engineering management occurred through an *operational* consideration of center of gravity. Fuel flow to the eight engines from the many thousands of gallons of fuel contained in an individual number of fuel cells filled virtually the entire wing. It was, literally, a flying gas tank. The fuel distribution system had been designed for automatic fuel feed in such a way that the center of gravity moved rearward with the depletion of fuel. While not critical on a conventional airplane with its tail leverage available to deal with turbulent air, in the minds of those of us thinking *operationally,* rearward travel of the center of gravity would further aggravate stability considerations on an aircraft with no tail. A forward center of gravity on any airplane enhances its behavior in turbulent air.

I brought this to the attention of my supervisor, suggesting that at that early point in final design determination, normal fuel flow could be designed to move the center of gravity forward with fuel depletion in flight. In a turbulent air situation, this would not stand as a great improvement, but it would help some.

My supervisor agreed and we presented the idea to the chief engineer and the head of the aerodynamics department—the department charged with center of gravity design considerations. We were overruled by the aerodynamics department's position to the effect that fuel system design had progressed to a point where such a change would be quite involved and not engender meaningful improvement.

This occasion did, however, open up my access to the chief engineer. With my supervisor's permission, I presented my Operational Flight Analysis management concept to him. He was very gracious and said that while the idea appeared to have merit, Northrop would not be interested in so sweeping a change in the engineering management system.

Back to square one, plodding along in the conventional wisdom context. However, about a year later my design engineering position, along with hundreds of other Northrop employees, changed quite dramatically.

In the Air Force test flying operation of the first pre-production model of this massive, eight-engine flying wing, they were doing stability tests over the Edwards Air Force Test Base in California's Mojave Desert. During one phase of the stability test, they lost control of the aircraft. Without the quality of longitudinal control normally applied in loss-of-control flight recovery situations, the massive flying wing tumbled into oblivion.

Shortly thereafter, following hundreds upon hundreds of millions of dollars poured into this program over the years, the Air force cancelled the entire flying wing program. Once more, I was out of a job. This time around, since earning the family's livelihood was first priority, I didn't even attempt to seek out another position with a big aircraft company. Only a couple of miles from my home, a small aircraft jet engine firm had just been established on the Van Nuys Airport in the San Fernando Valley. With no interest other than earning a living, I acquired a good paying design engineering position with them and in my spare time decided to formulate a new approach to the promotion of my concept.

What was needed, it seemed, was some specific focus on acquiring an ally *within* the Air Force. I elected to approach the Air Force Aero Medical Laboratory at Wright-Patterson Air Force Base in Dayton, Ohio. This Air Force organization was chartered to deal with pilot and crew "human engineering" considerations, probing key aspects of aircraft design. I wrote to Dr. Wayne Grether at the laboratory, enclosing a summary of the Operational Flight Analysis concept. Happily, the Aero Medical Laboratory was downright hungry for allies on the aircraft industry side of the fence. It seems they, too, were having great difficulty getting their message across to the aircraft industry. They immediately invited me to visit the laboratory for enlarged discussion.

How to get there. I couldn't afford such a trip. So, I phoned around to various airports, asking people I knew if they had any airplane that had to be ferried east somewhere near Dayton, Ohio. Bingo. Found one. They couldn't beat the ferrying charge, which was for free, so I had my trip east. Borrowing a few days of my vacation time, I took off for Ohio.

Upon arrival at my delivery point in Ohio, a one-hour bus ride found me in Dayton. At the laboratory, I walked into a very friendly atmosphere. Among other things, they were intrigued with the basic design principle of orienting aircraft operational needs to the unassailable dictates of flight in three dimensions of space and one dimension of time. This is a design principle which recognizes that pilot and crew are irretrievably committed to the dictates of detachment from earth, with often severe time limitations associated with performing all of the required operational mission tasks. It seems the laboratory was very much into time and motion studies associated with pilot and crew duties under the pressure of definitive time limitations—particularly under the psychological pressures of operational mission demands. Not that this aspect by any means covers the whole of Operational Flight Analysis, but the Aero Medical

Laboratory approach is pivotal. And they had been very frustrated over making so little progress in the aircraft designer's world.

Following additional discussion and agreement on a proposed organizational structure for an Operational Flight Analysis staff in aircraft industry engineering management, we discussed the primary reason for my visit to the Air Force Aero Medical Laboratory.

I explained that having thus far failed to make a connection with the aircraft industry, I was rewriting my proposal in rather blunt language and was seeking an ally in the Air Force to whom I might address the report. The report would be sent out with copies to several Air Force generals, Air Force agencies and to several large aircraft companies.

They thought that was a fine idea and promised their enthusiastic support if and when I made connection. Fair enough. Moreover, they agreed it might do some good, whatever the response. They also urged that I make a special point of sending a copy of my report to the Air Force's newly formed Deputy Inspector General's office for Aircraft Industry Technical Inspection and Flight Safety. I had not heard of this new office. The aero medical people said the Air Force was also becoming quite concerned over aircraft operational problems and unacceptable aircraft accident rates. Hence, the Air Force set up the Inspector General's new directorate at the highest level. The Deputy Inspector General's office was headed by a tough-minded, aircraft-industry-wise Major General Victor Bertrandias.

Now to return home and get down to a rather blunt rewrite of my previous too-gently written proposal. Getting home meant a cheap, tedious bus ride or calling on a former Air Force friend who had become a partner in a new airline. I called him and he said if I could get to Chicago, he would give me a ride to Los Angeles. Done.

As promised, I rewrote my proposal in quite blunt language and addressed it to Dr. Grether of the Aero Medical Laboratory, with copies to half-a-dozen major aircraft corporations, several Air Force generals and agencies and Deputy Inspector General Bertrandias. I signed the proposal as Captain, U.S. Air Force Reserve and Senior Design Engineer, Aircraft Industry.

Time passed with a few appreciative letters from some of the generals and Air Force agencies, in essence suggesting that I continue working with the Aero Medical Laboratory. But no access to financial support was suggested. There was no response at all from the aircraft industry.

Zilch! Zero! I was nowhere. I was nowhere. In disgust, I threw the last copy of my report into the fireplace. My wife grabbed the fire tongs and raked it out, saying that perhaps I expected too much too soon. I didn't really agree with her, but I filed my scorched report and dejectedly settled into the boring job I was in.

A month later, I received a most unexpected telephone call. Deputy Inspector General Bertrandias had chased me down by telephone and called me personally at my company's engineering office. He said he had studied my report and could I come out to see him. He was located only an hour's flight away at Norton Air Force Base in San Bernardino. I borrowed a friend's airplane and flew out to meet him that same afternoon.

Meeting him was an experience in itself. A hard as nails, gruff exterior, but gracious, too. After some get acquainted talk, he asked if I would return to active duty with his organization, promising in-depth statistical amplification of my report and then joining him in presenting same to General Twining, Chief of Staff of the Air Force and his staff. It was 1950. The U.S. was well into the Korean War at the time and simultaneously dealing with the new problems of the emerging jet age. He underscored what we both knew. The aircraft industry did not yet appear to properly embrace the Air Force's concern over the operational problems and accidents encountered with their aircraft. He said he now had the administrative clout to at least begin to deal with the problem.

We were, of course, in total agreement. However, while I was most respectfully appreciative of his offer, I was forced to point out, with my heart in my mouth, that not only could I not afford to return to active duty as a captain, but that with the rank of captain in a sea of majors and colonels surrounding him, I would most likely be put at a disadvantage in getting things done.

The general blinked, frowned, and then smiled at my respectfully delivered objection. "I can fix that," he said, "how about coming to work for me as an equivalent high-ranking civilian technical consultant?"... Sold! I quit my job immediately and moved the family to San Bernardino.

Parenthetically, returning to the Air Force in any capacity was farthest from my thought. But the fates sometimes conspire to take over and fit the missing pieces into one's objectives in life.

The early period in my new job was a bit tenuous. It seems the general had reproduced a hundred copies of my presentation and made it required reading across his organization—even before he had hired me. As one of the newest and highest ranking civilian consultants in his organization, the officers weren't quite clear on my relationship with the general and seemed to be holding me at arms length. While the general's senior officers all respected him, they seemed to be downright afraid of him.

My first month I was quietly involved in studying the organization structure and its mission, its accident investigation procedures, its aircraft industry relationships and its wealth of statistics on aircraft accidents and incidents. I was also included in his morning staff meeting comprised of abut twenty senior officers, two other consultants and myself.

The general hadn't spoken to me during that first month in other than a perfunctory manner. And then he really socked it to me. He overtly set me up in front of his entire staff.

After half-an-hour or so into the meeting, discussing the technical aspects of a recent accident investigation, General Bertrandias stated *his* position on the matter. Then, unexpectedly:

"Miner," asked the general, "what is your position on this?"

Taken by surprise, sitting on the opposite end of the conference table, should I offer him a wishy-washy, politically motivated response and violate my own doctrine, or tell the general what I thought?

"I'm sorry, Sir," I said, "but I disagree with you position."

There were a few suppressed gasps along the conference table.

All of the officers respected the general, but were somewhat afraid of his often hard-assed approach to things.

The general and I debated the issue for three or four minutes, and then he leaned forward in his chair, paused dramatically for at least ten seconds, and in the deadly quiet that prevailed, with his expression a bit grim, he said:

"Miner, your points are well taken and I agree with your position." He paused, leaning back in his chair with a half-smile, "But, Miner, I'm probably going to have to put you back in uniform and cut out this damn arguing."

Apparently, this wise old bird simply wanted his senior staff to endorse his reason for hiring me.

At that point, I was "in." A new friendliness obtained among the officers and it was now time for the general to assign me to aircraft accident investigation. The general had a fleet of B-25s for immediate travel to accident scenes with a major or colonel assigned as investigation team leader. I was assigned to various team leaders. As a civilian, having been required to resign my commission, I was not officially permitted to fly as pilot. But, happily, the team leaders were pleased to share their flying duties with me and I was able to enjoy keeping my hand in flying.

Surprising, even to me, the accident investigation situation revealed more than I had suspected as to the depth of the operational flight deficiency situation. As noted, we were at the time well into the Korean war and the emerging new jet age. Flight training had accelerated again, together with flight operations being conducted under less than ideal circumstances. Here are a few examples of problems encountered during accident investigation.

Jet engines, for one example. Since engine weight versus aircraft weight was always a point of design negotiation between engine manufacturers and airframe manufacturers. The engine designers at that time had decided on hundreds of light weight aluminum rotor blades in an engine turning many thousands of revolutions per minute. The problem was that ingestion by the engine's air intake duct of other than reasonably clean air—be it a bird or something sucked up off the runway—would strip the long row of aluminum rotor blades like a corn cob. The result was often an engine fire as the broken rotor blades piled up into an engine freeze. Needless to say, in the face of the accident record, it wasn't too long before the engine manufacturers changed over to steel rotor blades, increased engine weight notwithstanding.

Another surprise, even to me, was the extent of the poor accident and maintenance record of landing gear nose wheels on all aircraft types. Though operationally incorrect, the design textbook held that the main landing gear carried the load at the center of gravity and that the nose wheel was only an auxiliary wheel. In a non-flying, static load sense this was true. However, in an operational sense, with rough landings and often-poor ground taxiing conditions, the nose wheel was far from being merely an auxiliary wheel. And virtually every type of aircraft was experiencing unacceptable nose wheel problems. In the face of the Deputy Inspector General's glaring statistics, the textbook on nose wheel design was rewritten. Today, nose wheel failures are a rarity. I was glad to be instrumental in this change.

Another vital area of concern was the statistical evidence of flight control system failures, often due to the many built-in opportunities for control system malfunction as well as innocent maintenance mistakes due to incomplete design thinking from an operational point of view. More than on accident was attributed to the maintenance of hydraulic control systems wherein individual control system lines were identical in length and could easily and innocently be reinstalled so that the pilot's flight controls operated exactly opposite to their normal movement. The simple but vital operational fix, of course, was to make individual hydraulic lines slightly different in length so that they could only be installed correctly. Then, too, accident investigation also revealed many kinds of control system failures in flight that could have been precluded with more operational perspective in design. A related problem is the number of control system valves and other parts that are subcontracted to firms who have virtually no operational perspective at all. They are merely responding to some lower order design specification issued by the prime contractor with little or no appreciation of the end role played by their particular subcontracted part. Subcontracting to some large whole operational system is a major problem in its own right and will be discussed later.

While great strides have now been made in control system reliability, even recently we had the long standing Boeing 737 rudder control behavior problem. This was a condition wherein wrong rudder action was inadvertent and opposite to what the pilot would normally expect to deal with. The number of pilots and passengers killed in resulting accidents is well known. The number of times the pilot was barely able to overcome the problem and preclude an accident is not well known. The Boeing 737 errant rudder problem has at last been corrected.

Then, there were structural failures. One of the most interesting, to me, was the failure of the whole left wing on the Northrop F-80. Our accident investigation team was sent to Caribou, Maine, on a structural failure wherein the whole left wing broke off at its attachment point to the fuselage.

Impossible said the Northrop engineers. The pilot had to have been severely abusing the airplane to incite such an event. But unlike too many gruesome accidents, in which the pilot was killed, the pilot in this case successfully bailed out and was uninjured. He swore that he was not abusing the airplane and was only executing a tight turn at the time of the wing failure. Sadly, certain parties insisted he take a lie detector test that only confirmed he was telling the truth.

The broken wing had fallen into a large lake in one of Maine's state parks. Now, if accident investigation could be called pleasant, I would have to say this one was made pleasant by the fact that the very-much-alive pilot was with us in the boat as we searched for the broken wing. It was a bright sunny day in late September with the foliage colors of early fall most brilliant and the ambient temperature perfect. As we munched crab apples picked from an orchard next to the boat dock, we searched for and finally found the broken wing.

The wing had broken off from the fuselage center section at the wing attachment bolting flange, a machined flange involving more than a hundred attaching bolts. The wing had torn off on "the dotted line", so to speak. The flange had failed between the bolt holes. The wing was sent to the Air Force testing laboratory for analysis of the flange.

The problem was all too easily discovered by the people at the lab. For better understanding, note first that aluminum raw material is processed into usable material with grain flow—just as a piece of wood has grain flow. The design approach to applying aluminum material for maximum strength should be, of course, to machine the wing-attaching bolt holes along the grain flow of the material. In the case of the F-80 wing failure, the entire bolt flange had been manufactured cross-grain to the grain flow of the material, with each wing-attaching bolt trying to do its job across the weakest section of the material. The flange had failed between each bolt hole thus "tearing along the dotted line." A sad end to that short story.

I could go on and on with the myriad accident statistics generated by the Deputy Inspector General's office, but I will conclude this part of the discussion with the often nebulous factors which exist in dealing with those accidents too often prematurely charged to pilot error. There are many qualitative factors here, and the qualitative factors generated one of the more difficult aspects of accident investigation. That is, the qualitative situation can not always be quantified to a convincing degree.

Cockpit configuration, as noted in previous chapters, was the number one qualitative factor in accident investigation. That is to say, an often accident-inviting placement of a lever, switch, button, instrument or control might be functionally OK as an individual item. But in a poorly orchestrated mix of all of the items in the cockpit, the mix often stands as an open invitation to pilot error. Unfortunately, the cockpit all too often is a designer's "dart board" for whatever designer has some function to impose upon the pilot. The sequence and order of the pilot's needs are not always duly reckoned with.

Hence, one of the questions often asked by the accident investigator: Would a different and more operationally orchestrated cockpit configuration have served the operation in such a way as to reduce the tendency toward pilot error? The answer in so-called pilot error cases was often a resounding yes.

I was brought back once again to the urgency of implementing the key element of the Operational Flight Analysis proposal—design response to the fixed limitations of flight in three dimensions of space and one of time. With aircraft design ever increasing in complexity, together with accompanying sophistication of electronic equipment placed at the disposal of the pilot, the fixed, in-flight limitations imposed on the pilot are significant to say the least. This is particularly true under the increased pressures of night and instrument flying or combat operations, or both. Under these conditions, the pilot did not always have sufficient time to perform all of the operational duties required of him. Even the hottest and most experienced pilots were sometimes pushed beyond the limits of containability under fixed time limitations. This often resulted in an accident, or at best, a failed mission.

I recalled my discussions with the Aero Medical Laboratory people and their studied concern for the time and motion problem in flight, and their administrative difficulties in finding a voice in actual aircraft design. While this situation in the conduct of design has been improved somewhat in today's practices, we still have a long way to go.

In many borderline cases, accidents are still chalked up to pilot error. This fact tends not to be widely appreciated because even under today's somewhat improved situation, there are many accidents, incidents and failed operational missions that do not reach the level of "newsworthy." This is not to say that there are not accidents that are legitimately chargeable to pilot error, but only to point out that the tendency to charge off the accident to pilot error has often been a bit too hasty. Moreover, there are many accidents in which not only were the pilot and crew killed, but the wreckage was so completely destroyed that it often defied analysis... Much more yet to be done.

Some six or seven months following my immersion in the Deputy Inspector General's accident investigation activities, General Bertrandias decided we would make a joint presentation to the Chief of Staff of the Air Force, General Twining, and his generals and key staff people. This would be conducted in Washington in the War Room of the Pentagon. At General Bertrandias' direction, I would make the half-hour formal presentation with illustrative charts posted on the screen, and he would conduct the open session to follow.

The purpose behind the presentation was to lay the groundwork for new contract provisions in dealing with the aircraft industry. The intent was to specify a new working relationship with the industry in which operational flight analysis would be established as an integral and controlling part of the on-going design process. It was further specified that the group established to do this would be the primary contact point in Air Force coordination from design inception all the way through to Air Force flight test acceptance procedures.

At Pentagon presentation time, with a dazzling array of generals' stars sprinkled across the War Room, I wont deny that I was extremely nervous. The first few minutes of my part of the presentation were a bit stiff. But as the first chart flashed across the screen, I forgot myself and let my passion for the subject carry me through.

Now it was General Bertrandias' turn. It was fun to watch him conduct the open session, since he had no career axe to grind. He was on a mission and dealt very forcefully and pointedly with each issue raised by the audience. I do believe he left a lasting impression on the assembled group of Air Force leaders that morning. How soon all or some of our presentation might come to fruition was another matter, but General Bertrandias felt we had done our part.

Following the Pentagon presentation, and now with a deep involvement in accident investigation behind, the general moved me into the Aircraft Industry Technical Inspection side of his organization. Contacts with the aircraft industry were sometimes on an informal case by case basis. But most contacts were made in concert with the Air Force Aircraft Technical Inspection Board, which involved one vote from each of several Air Force agencies. The Air Force Inspector General's one vote was assigned to the Deputy Inspector General. The board's mission was to approve, disapprove or make recommendations on the aircraft designs of the various aircraft manufacturers doing business with the Air Force.

Because of my familiarity with the inner workings of the aircraft industry, General Bertrandias appointed me Chief of Technical Inspection Board Projects for his office. This assignment involved pulling together the various aspects of his one vote as it pertained to whatever aircraft design review we were scheduled to attend. I was to accompany the general's appointed colonel assigned to a scheduled board meeting as technical consultant to him.

What a difference it made to be working on the customer side of the fence… as opposed to struggling with the same kinds of ideas from way down in the bowels of the industry's engineering ranks. The aircraft industry design people didn't always respond properly to the Air Force board, but at least we had the clout to be listened to by the top people in the aircraft corporations we visited.

Of the many experiences encountered with the various aircraft firms, there is one experience in particular I would like to share. It was the early design and mock up phase of the Boeing B-52—still in service half-a-century later. I've selected this experience because it so clearly emphasizes the unreasoned power of the aerodynamics department in setting the course of design.

First, we have to back up a bit and look at Boeing's earlier, unsuccessful B-47 jet bomber. It went into production and Air Force service, but it did not last. It had a number of unsatisfactory design features from an operational point of view. The most glaring deficiency, thanks to Boeing's all powerful aerodynamics department, was a bubble canopy on this huge bomber wherein the pilot and copilot sat in tandem at some physical distance from one another; with other crew members below in the fuselage. The aerodynamics reasoned—without benefit of operational flight analysis intervention—that they must minimize the frontal area of the fuselage for maximum streamlining, ignoring fundamental operational flight principles.

Now, it must be underscored that operational flying of a large bomber is, in a manner of speaking, one-third stick and rudder and two-thirds cockpit and mission management. Indeed, pilot and copilot *must sit side by side* in order to deal directly with one another. Cockpit movements, hand signals, voice exchange without microphone, direct joint interface by pilot and copilot with the flight engineer and a myriad of nuances and qualitative factors entered in to make the B-47 cockpit and crew arrangement as far from operationally responsive as it could possibly be! I won't use some of the other adjectives that come to mind!

I mention the sad and very expensive story of the B-47 because of what occurred on the Air Force Board's visit to the B-52 inspection at the Boeing aircraft factory. Boeing designers had already the same basic, idiotic cockpit arrangement of the B-47 the B-52. Absolutely unthinkable from an operational point of view. I first discussed this privately with the colonel I was accompanying on this visit. As noted, he represented General Bertrandias' one vote on the inspection board. Since I was strictly in a consulting capacity to him, anything that was said to Boeing and other members of the Air Force Board would have to come from him. As a former bomber pilot himself, he was in complete agreement and he expressed our one vote accordingly.

The very slightly reduced aerodynamic efficiency in redesigning to a more blunt fuselage nose would hardly even be measurable on an aircraft of such huge scale as the B-52. Nonetheless, most of the other members of the board were persuaded by the fallacious arguments of the aerodynamics department.

We returned to our home base and took up the matter with General Bertrandias, who quickly agreed with our position. "I'll fix that one," he exclaimed somewhat vigorously. Calling his secretary, he said, "Get General Le May's office on the phone." General Le May, of course, was the commanding general of the Strategic Air Command and would be the recipient of the new B-52. He finally reached Le May, who was visiting the Edwards Air Force Test Base, a short, half-hour flight from our base. Without giving him any detail on the phone, other than stating we had a critical design situation to discuss regarding the B-52, our general made an appointment and we flew over the next morning.

This meeting was a joy to watch. After the colonel and I made our brief report on the Boeing meeting, our tough-minded general and an equally tough-minded General Le May lost no time getting down to the matter of the B-52 cockpit and crew arrangement. Le May, too, was surprised that the Air Force Aircraft Technical Inspection Board hadn't make a case for change.

Ahhh! Now to witness the unequivocal power of customer clout! General Le May was quite heated as he asked the office secretary to get the president of Boeing on the phone. The discussion was remarkably brief. Le May quickly spelled out the bottom line to Boeing's president: "Either redesign the cockpit configuration to a conventional side-by-side pilot and copilot arrangement, or, as commanding general of the Strategic Air Command, I simply will not buy the airplane!" Done!

Over the course of a year, we visited nearly all of the aircraft corporations doing business with the Air Force. This was very educational, to say the least. Notwithstanding differences of opinion from time to time, many suggestions were made and accepted by the designers.

At that point I was approaching a gratifying two years with general Bertrandias and I felt it was now time to rewrite my Operational Flight Analysis proposal still again, adding the wealth of information I had gathered, and try once again to identify with an aircraft industry career position.

I would miss the Deputy Inspector General's organization. Some fine relationships had been developed and there was great comradery among all of us, sharing as we did an unequivocal dedication to somehow participate in evolving operationally improved aircraft for the Air Force.

I discussed my thinking with the general who said that my intentions were not unexpected and that I had served him well. Even more particularly, he said I should now be armed to do more good on the aircraft industry side of the fence. He wrote me a fine letter of recommendation and a couple of months later we parted good friends.

At this point in an odyssey of discovery, it was time to sum up what I had learned since coming down from the mountains a few years earlier. Recalling fruitless efforts to reconnect with the aircraft industry at that time, the fates had conspired to thrust me, most unexpectedly, back into the Air Force.

I should note that in my often use of the term, "the fates conspired," I am unabashedly referring to God and angel intervention. Admittedly, as previously noted, I stumbled from time to time before agreeing with the fates. Nonetheless, the conspiring fates eventually won.

In any case, I was now armed with not only volumes of useful data confirming my OFA doctrine, but also a fresh perspective on the question...

"Why?"

Why was there such a wide gulf in operational system philosophy between the design engineers and scientists of the aircraft industry and the operational piople of the military? Answer: The widely disparate kinds of education and professional exposure experienced by these two basic groups.

That is to say, the education system at large is heavily biased toward specialization. The technological specialists, comprising over ninety-percent of the aircraft industry's engineering and science platform, have been taught largely to think in terms of parts and subsystems. Usually, they have been given little, if any, interdisciplinary education on that necessary quality of thinking which would enable the designer to reckon with integration of the parts and subsystems to work in concert with the operational whole of things. In short, this means that the design of many of the operational components of a final whole system are either force-fitted to the task they are expected to perform, or they are subject to very expensive post-production modification... or abandoned entirely.

The now old adage, "The whole is greater than the sum of the parts," even today receives little more than lip service in the education system at large. The lack of sufficient interdisciplinary training—or "generalist" training as opposed to "specialist" training—for all professionals lies at the heart of bringing together the design people and the operational people to evolve efficient whole systems at the outset of design.

The military operational people, on the other hand, including the National Aeronautics and Space Administration, while receiving some specialized training, of course, are primarily trained to think as interdisciplinarians—to think as generalists in terms of whole system planning to comprehensively defined operational tasks. That is: What is it that must be done to orchestrate a myriad of disparate parts, subsystems and human operators into a cohesive and efficient operational system?

The main point in all of this is that the aerospace people who design these system elements still have a long way to go before the interdisciplinary viewpoint takes hold. What must be overcome is that while the finally assembled total operational system usually gets the job done, this comes at an unacceptable cost. That is, the system all too often does its job with accidents, loss of human life, operational mission failures, vital loss of time and appallingly low cost-effectiveness.

Parenthetically, later chapters will offer the degree to which, even today, the above situation permeates the entire technological world, rapidly and dangerously diminishing the world's ecosystem. Now, this is not intended to put down the truly great accomplishments of the specialists of engineering and science. Rather, it is to underscore that the interdisciplinary imbalance between the specialists and the generalists, if not corrected by an errant education system, promises an unacceptable economic, sociological and ecosystem future. The specter of drowning in the specialist microcosm looms before us.

In reentering the aircraft industry, then, it would be most appropriate to remain sensitive to the various philosophical aspects and corporate political aspects of bringing these two philosophies together—eventually seeking to unite the specialists and the generalists at the outset of system design and throughout the design and development process. In turn, it would be appropriate to seek out and join ranks with that small cadre of outvoted researchers and educators who are working to make a more prominent place for interdisciplinary generalist training.

Hence, we sold the beautiful small home my wife and I had earlier built in the orange groves of Redlands, a small town just a few miles east of the air base. I then proceeded with submission of my rewritten OFA proposal to several major aircraft manufacturers... Here's hoping.

Chapter Six
Returning Again to the Big Corporation System
Swimming the Murky Waters of Corporate Politics

The most attractive response to my proposal came from the Lockheed Corporation. I met with both top engineering people and the brilliant engineering executive who also had extensive operational background and who had just been appointed Corporate Director of Military Relations and Development Planning. After several discussions with various executives, Lockheed felt that, initially, I should be placed on Chuck Thomas' newly established Military Relations Staff. Happily, we not only spoke the same language, but I found him intellectually honest and politically forthright—a prime requirement in an executive who would be directing my activities.

While my OFA proposal was the reason Lockheed was hiring me, they did not plan to implement it at that time. The general view among those I interviewed was that Lockheed should start hiring more people with my kind of background, with the intention of bringing about a gradual osmosis of operational perspective in the engineering organization at large.

Position secured, my wife and I embarked once again on the further practice of our favorite hobby, designing and building our homes. After settling temporarily in an apartment, we went on a search for a suitable building site. We found our site high on a hill in the residential community of Sherman Oaks, with a sweeping view of the entire San Fernando Valley. We designed a beautiful home with lots of plate glass embracing the view. The area offered kindly neighbors and pleasant living. We loved it.

In addition to general assignments by Chuck Thomas, which included visits to the Pentagon, making surveys and comments on potential areas of new business, getting acquainted with the Lockheed people, etc., he asked me a question regarding a more specific assignment. He asked what I thought about serving as military relations representative on Lockheed's new, single seat F-104. For a number of reasons this bothered me, but I didn't want to blow my new job by turning loose my maverickness. "Behave yourself," I muttered to myself.

When earlier shown the XF-104 experimental version, it was indeed a thing of great beauty. And make no mistake, it was fast. Fast! Fast! But, surprisingly, Lockheed was not aware of a few operational considerations during the design process. Among them, the perils of downward emergency ejection of the pilot's seat, a system that had been incorporated in the F-104 design.

The Air Force Test Center, in exhaustive tests of a downward pilot seat ejection system with live subjects, clearly revealed the problem. With downward ejection seats installed in a large test airplane, it was revealed that even under ideal conditions, the downward ejection explosive force was so great that the pilot's arms and legs could not always be kept within the narrow boundaries of the seat ejection envelope. Broken limbs were the net result.

Somehow, those findings had not reached Lockheed's design engineering people. Such findings would have reached them had an Operational Flight Analysis organization existed within the engineering department. In any case, the F-104 pilot ejection seat system would have to be changed to upward ejection, wherein the pilot's arms and legs tended to stay naturally within the narrow ejection envelope.

Fortunately, so early in my new job, I didn't have to use up my limited political capital in making this point. I could have aggravated the design engineers, having this major change thrust upon them by the new kid on the block. I had only to urge them to call the Air Force Test Center before the Air Force had to deal with Lockheed on a very expensive post-production modification. The F-104 seat ejection system was changed to upward ejection.

Another F-104 problem was landing gear design. Both main wheels retracted forward, which was good, since the air stream assisted quick landing gear extension. But the nose wheel on the airplane had been designed to retract rearward, which made for sluggish nose wheel extension against the air stream. Again, fortunately, I did not have to make that point. Lockheed's test pilot pointed out that the F-104 was so hot that he "dirtied up the airplane" with landing gear extension as late in the landing approach process as possible. The nose wheel design was changed to forward retraction for maximum air stream assist on quick landing gear extension.

Finally, I jokingly asked the competent, but nonflying engineer who was giving me the tour of the XF-104, "I see those little fins sticking outside of the fuselage, but where are the wings?"

He laughed and said, "That's the way it is. The short wings, if you will, are one of the reasons the F-104 goes so fast."

For a change, I again kept my mouth shut and did not voice my opinion to the effect that the airplane might prove to be too hot an airplane for even the better Air Force pilots. In any case, no way would Lockheed consider adding wing spread at that near-production juncture. Time and cost wise, the aerodynamic, structural and manufacturing tooling considerations would have been prohibitive.

In talking Lockheed's star test pilot, Tony Levier, he informally acknowledged that only the Air Force's best pilots should fly that airplane. And he was speaking only of clear weather, daytime flying. Putting instrument approaches to landing under a low ceiling, or night landings, into the equation was still another matter, further compounding the risk of flying this very hot airplane.

The F-104 might well prove to be a pilot killer. I was not a bit happy over the prospect of representing this airplane to the Air Force. But I said nothing, since the F-104 had not yet started to roll off the production line. Some other assignment, hopefully, would relieve me of that unwelcome task.

I should note here that later on, when finally delivered to the Air Force, the F-104, very sadly, did indeed turn out to be a pilot killer. It acquired a terrible accident record. It was not successful. Quite a few more feet of wingspread and a little less speed would have made it a fine airplane.

However, I must not leave the bad history of this one airplane without making special note of Lockheed's long history of good airplanes. Whatever the design and development problems they may have had along the way, they have served well into the past as well as the present. The point is, the F-104 situation was a very clear example of the vital need for an authoritative OFA doctrine within the aircraft designer's immediate domain.

But circumstances do change. To my great relief, the fates were conspiring once again and I was soon to receive a fine new position. My very much-appreciated director, Chuck Thomas, was being moved to greater things and his immediate small staff dispersed across the other departments.

Unknown to me was Thomas' more than casual effort to see me properly placed elsewhere in the corporation. His good friend, Willis Hawkins, who was one of the engineering executives I had earlier interviewed, and who had read my OFA proposal a year earlier, had just been promoted as Chief Engineer of Lockheed's newly formed Missiles and Space Company. He said he now had the authority to introduce new concepts into the engineering management system, and would I like the position of division head over a couple of hundred engineers and scientists, which would also include the necessary wide range of operational, human engineering, logistics and air technical intelligence skills that would be involved. He, like Thomas, was also a pilot and very sensitive to the aircraft industry's somewhat inadequate operational system thinking.

I eagerly said yes. I didn't even bring up the salary question. I was automatically given a substantial raise and was also included in Lockheed's executive bonus program. The fates had a plan. I just didn't know about it. While, at first, I asked myself what I was doing in the missiles and space side of things instead of piloted aircraft, the answer came quickly. The planning, management and design approach to missiles and space vehicle development was in principle, very much the same as that spelled out in my OFA proposal. The same basic elements were simply applied in the operational system in a different manner.

Whether missile of piloted aircraft, each whole operational system was comprised of the same basic subsystem elements—the flying element, the surface based element, and the human crew with the operational system command element.

Now begins the rather tentative approach to one of the murky aspects of corporate politics. Whereas Chuck Thomas' military relations staff readily yielded good relationships, the brilliant, but also politically astute Chief Engineer Hawkins, cautioned me on possible language barriers with the engineering people which could pose obstacles to friendly communications.

"What do you mean?" I asked, somewhat anticipating his answer.

"We are, indeed, in complete agreement as to the scope of your new division, and that you will be hiring a number of experts directly out of the military domain. However," he cautioned, "the cloistered career patterns of the design room engineers and scientists of this decade of the nineteen-fifties will find them nervous over language heretofore not commonly used in the design room."

"In light of this," smiled Hawkins, "sneak up on the engineers with your necessary new language base. Let them feel their way into a new way of life in the corporate engineering environment of the future."

He paused for a moment and said, "For example, instead of calling your new Operational Flight Analysis Laboratory by that name, let's call it The Problems Room. And wherever you can, avoid the terms 'Human Engineering', 'Air Technical Intelligence and Logistics'. For example," he closed somewhat apologetically, "refer to logistics as packaging and movement of men and materials."

"Whew! I'll give it my best shot, Chief," I smiled. And so I got on with hiring and organizing a full spectrum of engineering, scientific and operational management systems people required to flesh out the OFA doctrine. This also included a New Concepts Research Staff, embracing both interdisciplinary generalist skills and scientific specialist skills.

During this initial organizational phase, a most interesting corollary opportunity presented itself. It seemed that the Dean of Engineering at the University of California at Los Angeles was growing quite concerned over the general problem of insufficient emphasis on the interdisciplinary aspects of all engineering activities. In turn, he invited key technical executives from various corporations in the Los Angeles area to join him in a continuing committee effort to address this growing problem as it bore on curriculum improvement. In the decade of the fifties, this was far-sighted thinking. Yet, if Dean Boelter were alive today, he would be justified in observing how little real progress had been made in interdisciplinary and generalist technical training. In any case, as it turned out, Chief Engineer Hawkins, who had also received Dean Boelter's invitation, was unable to work the invitation into his schedule. So, he sent me in his place. Obviously, I was delighted to be involved in a subject about which I felt so strongly.

Our first major thrust in the new Lockheed Missiles and Space Company was to build the working facility. Initially, some very large hangars on the Van Nuys Airport in San Fernando Valley were secured and converted to appropriate technical and manufacturing facilities. This was followed, of course, by an intense effort to respond to the opportunities for new business beyond the few small contracts Lockheed had earlier secured.

My major involvement during the early period with the new company was in support of Lockheed's intense effort to win the multi-billion dollar prime contract on the Navy's new sea-based Polaris missile system. This was a program I could honestly believe in as truly necessary to the security of our country in the decades leading up to the eventual end of the cold war with the Soviet Union. Deterrent warfare through the strength of our weapon systems was the name of the game.

We were barely into our proposal effort in response to the Navy's preliminary specification of a sea-going strategic missile system when our embryo Operational Flight Analysis Laboratory—the "Problems Room"—came into play.

In the center of the large room we had placed a fifteen-foot round table with a polar projection map of the Northern Hemisphere. On the map we posted key target areas in the Soviet Union and the range requirements of Polaris missile ships patrolling the North Atlantic Ocean. On the walls were large scale detail maps and preliminary sketches of the logistic components of the total system, with emphasis on sketches of possible launching platforms on the deck of the ship.

Since this would be a surface ship, we also posted expected sea states for various times of the year in the northern latitudes. Should a real wartime situation arise, the missiles would be required to launch immediately, of course, regardless of weather or rough sea conditions at the time.

During our preliminary proposal discussions, we examined the launching situation in more detail, and took a hard look at the logistics of handling such exotic fuels as red fuming nitric acid, along with other troubling operational factors in a severe weather and rough sea state-launching situation. Some of us in those early preliminary design conferences had our doubts on the feasibility of such a system. Launching a long range, liquid fueled ballistic missile from a surface ship in a rough sea seemed unthinkable.

What to do? It was immediately obvious that the only stable launching platform at sea would be a submarine. True, but still unthinkable from the logistic standpoint of exotic liquid fuels. So what ought we to do to meet the strategic missile range requirement of up to several thousand miles? The only answer, of course, was a solid propellant fuel, up-scaled from the type of solid fuel rocket motors used in short range, small missiles. Impossible, most of the engineers and scientists first exclaimed. Solid-fueled missiles were practical only for short-range missiles, they protested.

Not necessarily, our OFA staff offered, but we did not have enough voting clout to overcome the resistance of those engineers and scientists who would be doing the actual design work. Moreover, some of them were a bit too politically hasty in simply wanting to give the Navy a proposal responsive to what they were asking for. That is, without giving sufficient attention to the practical whole of the operational problem.

In any case, my staff and I did not have sufficient scientific depth in solid propulsion chemistry and related mathematical aspects to argue other than operational feasibility issues. But I certainly knew of an engineer-scientist who could respond to the whole of the operational problem, namely, their boss, Irv Culver, head of the Design Engineering Division.

At this point, I must introduce one of my most respected associates. Irv Culver was true genius in the greatest sense of that term. He was engineer, scientist and pilot. His brilliance was exceeded only by his admirable self-effacing personality. Nothing phased him. He was always polite, even in the face of ignorance and I had never seen him angry, even with good cause. He had been hand picked for the job by another very bright man, our mutual boss, Chief Engineer Hawkins.

Upon Culver's return from a trip, I rallied him to the operational problem. After he and I discussed the problem privately in the OFA room, he said, "I agree with you completely, but give me a couple of days for some preliminary thought and we'll talk to the people involved." Then, speaking to the assembled group of scientists and engineers, he offered a coherent rationale for why he thought a submarine-launched, solid propellant long-range ballistic missile was feasible. We presented this to the Chief Engineer and with his endorsement joined the Navy in a further study of the problem. The Navy then joined us, together with our propulsion motor subcontractor and the submarine people to confirm and move forward with the Lockheed-proposed approach to the Polaris missile system.

This was followed by our meeting in Washington with Admiral Raborn, head of the entire Polaris program, his staff, the submarine manufacturer and representatives of the Navy's submarine fleet. At that meeting, a decision was made on the feasible elongation of a nuclear submarine in terms of the number of missiles per submarine that would be structurally and operationally practical.

Basic approach now confirmed and agreed upon, the Navy threw us a giant curve ball. They required a Polaris program, which normally would require ten years to complete, to be completed in four years. This was tough, since the state-of-the-art was being pushed to its limits at that time. Admiral Raborn pointed out that this was necessary in order to respond properly to the government's intelligence estimate of the cold war threat as foreseen at that time.

With no other choice, in the light of Lockheed management's eagerness to acquire a long-term, multi-billion dollar contract, we said, "Yes, we can do it."

Overlapping all of this was the corporate decision to build the permanent Lockheed Missiles and Space Company facility up north in the Silicon Valley area. A large tract of land was acquired near San Francisco Bay on the perimeter of the town of Sunnyvale; accompanied with a rigorously accelerated building construction program. In 1956, they started moving personnel to our new northern location.

I was scheduled to move in mid-1957. Hence, my wife and I bought a beautiful one-acre home site in the Los Altos Hills area a few miles west of the new Lockheed plant. Once again we designed our home and had it built to our specifications. It was expected to be ready in the summer of 1957, our planned moving date.

In the meantime, the nature of my own division as a supporting organization to other departments, coupled with intense involvement in the Polaris program, found me with offices in both north and south plants; that is, until the southern plant would finally be phased out.

At least I had the fun of flying the small twin engine airplane Lockheed had acquired. We had hired a company pilot who was fully current on his instrument flying, but he was always kind enough to let me do the flying when I was one of the passengers. While I still had my own multi-engine and instrument ratings, I could not consider myself viably current on instruments for flying commercial passengers. In any case, these were fun breaks and served as a useful reminder on the unequivocal nature of three dimensions of space and one dimension of time when detached from earth.

As we moved into early 1957, the severity of seventy and eighty-hour weeks were taking their toll on some of us—particularly when adding in the buzzing back and forth between north and south offices. In some respects, this was more difficult than the war situation. In addition to the work overload itself, there were squabbles and disagreements that were not always easily resolved. Our hiring program was intense and we were to a large extent working with hundreds of engineers and scientists whose motivations and attitudes were yet to be juggled into viable working relationships. All of this, combined with the design and construction supervision of our new home, finally caught up with me.

One early evening during the construction of our home, after the workmen had left for the day, I had leaned over to check a framing measurement and, most unexpectedly, fainted. When I regained consciousness, I made it back to the hotel. The next day, not feeling myself at all, I flew back to our home in Sherman Oaks and went to bed for nearly a month. The doctor defined it as nervous exhaustion, just short of a nervous breakdown... Who, me?

This would never do. I was only thirty-seven. What's going on here? I spent a month giving this some very serious thought. Unlike the war situation, for all of its dangers and emotional pressures, the war was lived in an atmosphere of high comradery, teamwork and love of fellow man. Sadly, this was not true in the high pressured, politically driven corporate world of technology—particularly when one was assigned program evaluation tasks that often flew in the face of the conventional technological wisdom. This "wisdom" the psychologists often define as "group think"—a situation wherein the strong-minded people take a position and the less strong-minded simply follow along.

I came to realize, in the extremely high pressured Polaris program, that I was experiencing much emotional turmoil in my role as evaluator of other peoples' work. Those who were being evaluated, no matter how graciously approached, were often openly hostile. Chief Engineer Hawkins jokingly called me his "technical cop." I have a good sense of humor, but that "technical cop" tag I did not find one bit humorous. While agreeing with what I was doing, Hawkins fell into the role of placator between the line technical people and myself—and I took the heat. I would have much-preferred working directly in a line position rather than staff and be directly involved in getting things done—as in my previous positions—rather than critiquing the work of others. But this was denied me all of my years with Lockheed. Moreover, comradery and team spirit seemed to be lacking across the board. Oh, yes, personal friendships and certain alliances were formed, but the overall corporate political undercurrents were rough on both line and staff people. While there was honest dedication on the part of many, there was no wartime-like comradery and team spirit. It was simply worse if one were in a staff role. Nor was I alone in getting ill over it all. Others suffered as well, including a number of heart attacks.

For all of Chief Engineer Hawkins' suggestions on using military operational systems language cautiously in the design room during the era of the 1950's, such language was often unavoidable. This was particularly the case when new management systems were installed to reflect the real world. The management system we devised to meet the fiercely tight program schedule for Polaris was strictly based on an operational flight metaphor. It placed equal emphasis on the (1) Flying elements of the system, (2) The surface based elements of the system and (3) The logistics and operational crew systems at all levels as visualized through to a Polaris submarine on patrol, ready to fire on command. It was often difficult to persuade the designers to the subtle system integration influences that arose in sweeping from the missile to the submarine and to the people who are operationally charged with making the system work.

In my growing fatigue and slow recovery from my illness, I

became rather short tempered with people who were often more hardheaded than myself. Even though I believed in the validity of the weapon system I was working on, I was beginning to question the purpose of it all, since so much of family life and the joys of living were being postponed. Moreover, my work attitude seemed to have lost its buoyancy.

The overall situation after the permanent move to the north became even less appealing, largely because of sweeping organizational changes. The company, in effect, was divided into two separate companies—the missile division in one facility and the space division in another facility with central management in a middle facility. Entirely separate organizations were formed, each with its vice-president reporting to the president in central management.

In this process, the engineering organization was disbanded and former Chief Engineer Hawkins move to higher things in central management. The OFA Laboratory, for all of its proven worth, even in its embryo form, was never reconstituted after the company moved north. The concept fell apart except for the request that I keep the OFA program evaluation process alive on my staff.

My organization of five-hundred engineers and scientists was disbanded and fanned across the two new divisions of the company; except for fifty people retained on my staff. I was appointed Director of Planning, Program Evaluation and Management Systems Development, reporting to the vice-president of the missiles division, Stan Burriss. At least Stan was a compatible supervisor who had earlier joined Lockheed as an engineer with a strong Navy background in engineering and operational testing. He was very simpatico with my operational philosophy. My office was next to his and we became good friends.

One aspect of things he did not like—and I didn't much like it either—was the president's prerogative of overriding Burriss and calling me into private meetings with him for an independent evaluation of how things were *really* progressing on the Polaris program. Politically, this often left me between a rock and a hard place—even though I always reported the results of these meetings to Burriss. But that's the way it was.

In this context, I recall one particularly sticky political issue for me. Company President Gene Root had called me for another private meeting about a month before the scheduled first flight of the Polaris prototype missile from a ground-based launching pad. These private meeting s were usually held in his home on Sunday evening after my wife and I had Sunday dinner with him and his family. We then met in his den while the wives visited in the living room.

He started our meeting by saying that by some miracle it appeared we were going to launch this advanced state-of-the-art prototype missile on schedule. In thinking of the near-impossibility of this schedule, his question was, "Are we really going to launch on schedule with a missile that works?"

Now, for me, here is the sticky part. I said, "Yes, we'll launch on schedule, but, in my opinion, the missile will go every which way but up."

Root's eyes opened wide. "That's not the way I've been hearing it. What do you mean? Is this just a judgement call on your part, or do you have a foundation for your opinion?"

I pointed out first that one of my program evaluation prerogatives was to install observers from my own staff in various subcontractor organizations. I had my representative at the propulsion subcontractor's facility making some special tests on the material specified for our "jetavator" controls.

Parenthetically, the jetavator, in principle, is not unlike the elevator on an airplane. The elevator controls the airplane by changing the angle of the elevator into the airstream. In the case of the jetavator, its surface is mounted so that it turns into the rocket nozzle blast on command, shifting the direction of the blast as required to steer the missile.

I explained to President Root that in the course of examining the drawings for the jetavator installation, it seemed to me, intuitively, that with an expected rocket gas temperature running much higher than that which we had previously reckoned with, that the jetavator mounting and hinge pin mass was too light and could not possibly hold up for the amount of flight time required before normal rocket motor burn out. I explained that I had my representative at the subcontractor's facility run endurance tests on a comparable metal mass at elevated temperature. He had confirmed my suspicions on our jetavator design.

But in a staff meeting with Stan Burriss and the design engineers, I further explained, the designers were not persuaded that my evaluation of the jetavator situation was correct. Unfortunately, Burriss sided with the engineers, who were in "group think" and had a large and persuasive vote.

"If all you say is true," said President Root, "then we must advise the Navy and extend the flight test schedule."

"No, Sir," I respectfully protested, "I urge we not tell the Navy for psychological reasons. That is, most of the engineers and scientists feel that the Polaris schedule is unrealistic anyway, and that if we were to announce a delay, we would simply enter into a contract schedule overrun—with the usual variety of excuses offered to the military customer." I further observed, "If the criticality of the Polaris schedule dictated by the Navy is for real, and we cancel the schedule for the first prototype flight, then we are going to be faced with some serious questions from the Navy regarding our contracted promises. If we miss this first scheduled milestone, then the Navy will start to wonder if succeeding key program milestones might also tumble."

"But schedule notwithstanding," asked Root, "Why would we go ahead with the first launch if you're reasonably sure of failure?"

"Because it will be *on schedule*. As you so well know, Gene, the military customer always tends to accept early test failures on new missiles as part of the game. And, while such failures are disappointing, of course, they are not usually politically damaging—particularly when pushing the state-of-the-art to the extremes found in the Polaris missile. On the other hand," I reiterated, "the Navy would not likely be at all friendly toward our not keeping our first schedule promise on this highly unique program."

I went on to point out that my staff and I had been working with the behavioral science people at Stanford University (our next door neighbor in Palo Alto) and that we had concluded that the Polaris program, with its inviolate schedule mandates, is, uniquely enough, a behavioral problem. That is, engineers and scientists cannot be asked how much time would be required to achieve a certain design or invention objective. They will have to be *management-directed* to achieve certain goals by decree—notwithstanding their occasional protests of "the impossible."

"If, indeed," I continued, "the first Polaris launch fails as reasonably expected, then the technical staff would most likely get the idea that both the Navy *and Lockheed* are deadly serious about the Polaris schedule."

Root then agreed we would not advise the Navy of our concerns, but said he wanted to talk to Burriss and myself right after the test. "After all," he said as he closed the meeting, "the damn thing might work in spite of your reasonable concerns." He thanked me for the meeting and after nightcaps with our wives, Rosemary and I went home.

The launch day of the prototype Polaris missile occurred on schedule. Sadly, this first Polaris was hardly off the launch pad before the jetavators disintegrated. But the technical staff now had the message. The Polaris system would be held to a schedule, notwithstanding the rather cavalier attitude of some engineers and scientists who felt their own views of required design time had been abused. Their attitudes were now mandated to the new order of things.

The new control system design was based on rotable rocket blast nozzles. This meant steering the missile by changing the blast direction of the entire nozzle blast, rather than by insertion of jetavators into the blast. Since subsequent flight test schedules had yet to be announced, and would be adjusted to fit the key milestones of the program, the overall design and development effort would be kept moving in the right direction... and with no further questions on the imperatives of schedule integrity.

As to planning and scheduling management systems, the necessary new approaches were to be formalized. As prime missile contractor, Lockheed was required to devise entirely new management concepts as required to mature the whole of the operational system on schedule.

As Director of Planning, Program Evaluation and Management Systems, it fell to my staff to handle Lockheed's end of developing the new management system. Enter again the often frustrating political intrigue that attended the integration of diverse subcontractor management systems associated with not only Lockheed's spectrum of subcontractors on the missile proper, but those related to the submarine and logistic systems required to put the whole of the operational Polaris system on sea patrol.

The Navy called for a management system named "Program Evaluation and Review Technique," known by the acronym "PERT." They also awarded a contract to Harvard University to develop the system in concert with Lockheed. The Harvard end of the effort was headed by Professor Sterling Livingston.

The basic concept was to develop a "critical path" of key program milestones, into which would be fed a myriad of parts and subsystem design, development and manufacturing activities to form a giant network of all participants and their respective schedules. Agreeing with the basic concept, we then fell into a conceptual struggle over how the program would be implemented.

The Harvard approach was that of asking each designer to estimate the time required to complete his particular assigned task, and then feeding the collective estimates of the designers into the PERT critical path of milestone events. Two fundamental considerations invalidated that approach.

First, as earlier noted, we had determined—supported by the Stanford behavioral science people—that management, in the Polaris schedule context, does not ask the designer for his estimate of time required to complete his task. He must respond to a management-directed schedule, not to the traditional time-estimating methodology.

Sample tests of PERT, asking each designer for his own estimate of design time, found that when fed into a critical path milestone, the collective time estimates of the designers involved in the PERT test far exceeded the real schedule time available.

The second fundamental consideration to be challenged was that of initially addressing PERT only to the missile design and development program. That is, at the outset, PERT should also address the downstream schedule implications of production tooling and manufacturing considerations, submarine system integration, and the logistics of achieving operational system readiness of the system as a whole.

Our Lockheed position regarding the PERT critical path management network was based on the principle of operational system wholeness. That is: Operational weapon system design and schedule planning is properly approached only by hypothesizing the operational end point first, with all system elements identified and integrated to a point of operational readiness. The critical path network of key milestone events is then developed rearward through the various logistics, manufacturing, development and design phases to the first milestone event on the critical path network.

Moreover, since traditional development practice tended to find the surface based element of a system seriously schedule-delinquent, we proposed that all operational elements of the Polaris system be a part of the PERT critical path network schedule at the outset of the program.

The above point ins a most vital one. It had long been characteristic of the aerospace industry to charge ahead with the flying element of a weapon system without due regard for design influences dictated by integration of the flying element into a combat-ready operational system. Most of these downstream logistics, operational crew and environmental ambience influences were foreseeable as to their early effects on the design effort. But traditional emphasis on the flying element without sufficient regard for downstream system integration influences has led, cumulatively, to billions upon billions of dollars of retrofit expenses *after* placing the flying element into the completed operational system—expenses that could have been avoided through an appropriate holistic system philosophy of design.

Another consideration for the reader: The points in the above observation apply not only to the aerospace industry, but to the entire delinquent planning philosophy of those governmental and industrial agencies charged with reconciling and planning for the infrastructure needs of an unprecedented population explosion. This consideration will be heavily emphasized in the last chapter and the epilogue.

Obviously, we had to change earlier preconceived concepts as to the approach to the new PERT management system. We then had to convince all participants in this vast program that all subsystem considerations were to be studied simultaneously in order to ascertain intra-system design influences as early as possible in the design process.

Harvard University was quite far downstream on another approach, but some good luck intervened. It so happened, quite by coincidence, that Professor Livingston and I were each giving independent management systems lectures to the American Management Association on the same day in New York. We both had the evening free and he invited me to dinner at the Four Seasons Restaurant. After an excellent dinner accompanied by pleasant, informal exchange of our differing views of PERT, we continued our discussion while strolling the streets of New York for the better part of the evening.

That productive evening was followed by a subsequent meeting in California in our home, involving only Livingston, Burriss and myself. We didn't get it all sorted out at that time, but things were gradually moving onto the broader track, including productive input by Professor Livingston.

I should also note that while the PERT system was yet far from perfect, it did force a continuing broad-based view of the entire program by all participants. It is also interesting to note that in the course of our PERT development, the National Aeronautics and Space Administration (NASA) had heard of our PERT efforts through the Navy. While NASA already had a good grasp on what operational system integration was all about, they, nonetheless, in the 1960's time period, sent the NASA staff of famous German rocket scientist, Werner Von Braun, to Lockheed for a comprehensive PERT briefing.

To what extent NASA adopted that system I do not know. But suffice to say, NASA's record on such ambitious operational undertakings as the manned flight to the moon and return are more than spectacular—though not, they admit, without the great difficulty they experienced in bringing together the disparate views of many subcontractors and system analysts.

As the Polaris missile system progressed, I was directed to start spending more program evaluation time with the submarine people at the submarine works in Groton, Connecticut. This, too, was quite a revelation to an aircraft person such as myself. The Polaris submarine was, indeed, quite a ship.

But as I soon found out, a submarine is not a ship, as the Navy representative pointed out at lunch one day.

"No, no," he laughingly exclaimed. "No matter the size, a submarine is a boat! Always a boat!"

"Well, OK," said this Air Force clod. "A boat it is." But it was quite a boat. Not only huge in scale out of the water, but unbelievably complex in it's highly condensed systems and subsystems. System integration considerations loomed all the more forcefully in my mind.

Time moved on, my brief illness now well behind me, I started taking inventory of where I was going, career wise. Though Stan Burriss had cooled our friendship a bit in the light of my "command performances" with President Root, particularly after the failure of the first test flight, we were more or less on good terms. But, politically, he had filled the unfilled position of Deputy Head of the Missiles Division with a retired Navy officer, who, though bright enough, didn't have a clue on the intricacies of corporate management or on design engineering and manufacturing procedures.

I was very disappointed. I felt I had more than earned that position. But on the other hand, I was ex-Air Force, not ex-Navy. Burriss was ex-Navy. Moreover, Admiral Raborn was very pleased with Burriss' appointment of a prominent ex-Navy officer as deputy. The political atmosphere for Lockheed was obviously enhanced. Make no mistake, the good-old-boy syndrome is very much alive and a career force to be reckoned with.

I should also make note here of the career political hazards in protracted involvement in any kind of top-level evaluatory position—or as "technical cop," to use former Chief Engineer Hawkins' annoying term. Even if one were not a maverick, the constant critiquing of other peoples' work eventually finds one on politically thin ice. This makes for severely inhibited career opportunities. One's image becomes that of a person who doesn't get along too well with people. After nearly ten years in such a role, I now felt my career potential at Lockheed was at and end. It was time to move on.

The Boeing Aircraft Company in Seattle had just been awarded the Air Force contract for the then new, underground, silo-based, long-range ballistic missile—named "Minuteman." In the light of Polaris' promise with advanced state-of-the-art solid propellant motors, Minuteman was also to be solid propellant powered. I speculated they might be interested in my Polaris experience.

I wrote to the Boeing Missiles Division, inquiring to that end. They were, indeed, most interested and very quick to respond to my inquiry. I felt I should advise Burriss of my intentions. He understood and wrote me a good letter of recommendation. I took some vacation time, packed up the family, and we were off to Seattle for an interview.

The interview was very successful—even upon my vigorous assertion that any kind of program evaluation role or staff advisory role was completely unacceptable. I insisted that a line role on the direct execution of task management was the only position I would consider. They agreed, offered a substantial salary adjustment commensurate with that of Deputy Program Director and it appeared a Boeing position would be quite acceptable. I asked for a week to digest all that had been discussed, including tentative promises, and that I would respond to their offer at that time.

While we were in the Seattle area, my wife and I searched for a suitable home. We found a beautiful small home on Mercer Island with a gorgeous view of the Cascade Mountains. We placed a refundable deposit hold on this home, agreeing on probable finalization in ten days. We then took off for our home in Los Altos, which had already been sold on a ninety-day escrow basis.

But before I even had a chance to think over the Boeing offer, a courtesy telephone call was made between the Boeing president and Lockheed's President Root to make sure that Boeing's hiring me was not in conflict with Lockheed's thinking. Such courtesy calls between companies regarding personnel were not uncommon in the industry.

In my case, surprisingly, President Root took it upon himself to say that Lockheed had other plans for me—without first discussing it with me. He then transferred me directly to his own office as a Research and Development Consultant in central management. I was now out of the Missiles Division and this new assignment seemed to have possibilities. For me this was particularly true since I was no longer in that most tiresome and emotionally unrewarding role of evaluating the work of others. After nearly ten years with Lockheed in staff roles, I was truly bone weary and unhappy, notwithstanding having scored a few useful points along the way.

The transfer to Root's office looked promising enough to put aside the idea of looking elsewhere for a position. My wife and I moved temporarily into an apartment and selected another home site. Always a joy for us, we designed and built another home in the Los Altos hills with a distant view of San Francisco Bay.

Two of the initial assignments in my new role I particularly enjoyed. The first of these was to take a long-term view of economic growth in both expected defense contract areas and in yet unsurveyed new opportunities in non-defense areas. Emphasis was to be placed on non-defense opportunities that might exist on a long-range basis.

This effort was to include economic growth and environmental aspects which were always of interest to me, though I did need outside expertise to fill in those research areas with which I was not familiar. I was authorized to put together a small study group comprised of economics, demographic and ecology experts from Stanford Research Institute, together with our own system analysts.

In this nearly six-month study, we found ourselves synthesizing economic growth parameters which, while somewhat known in limited circles, were heretofore ignored or so poorly structured that they found no place in the real world—the practical world of dealing with explosive economic growth. That is, valuable data were simply languishing in various government archives and research foundation libraries. We found this sad situation to be largely due to fragmentation and lack of integration of piecemeal studies in terms of the whole of things.

We took note of hundreds of nonprofit research foundations who were studying various aspects of problem areas we were interested in. Most alarming to me was the finding that interdisciplinary effort among foundations working in similar areas was almost nonexistent. One foundation president I talked to apologetically admitted to this, explaining that most foundations were too busy guarding their own turf because of the often fierce competition for nonprofit research funding... Not entirely true, one would hope.

In any case, we extracted information we could use from a few of these foundations, and then proceeded to synthesize this information via direct interviews with a wide spectrum of industries operating in the real world of national and international commerce. Surprisingly enough, we found that both the research foundation people and most industrial firms were making long term projections of various components of economic growth, but they were not integrating their projections to form a cohesive, holistic statement. In short, they did not offer a picture to government planning agencies that would dramatize the urgency of immediate priority attention to the then emerging new specter of hyper-explosive economic growth.

Our Lockheed study group's initial reaction to this situation was almost simple minded in our unbelief that such a monstrous situation was going unattended. But we could find no evidence at the time to the effect that Malthus' classical historical thesis on population growth versus subsistence demands was being put forward in a contemporary context.

Hence, as a first step toward synthesis of hundreds of data

fragments, we set up a huge six by ten-foot chart with the whole twentieth century as a viewing window. The vertical scale on the chart represented both population growth and subsistence demands expressed as a percentage of growth from the beginning of the twentieth century.

For graphic clarity, we arbitrarily elected the midway point in the century as a hundred-percent growth point for all population and subsistence demands. Again, for graphic clarity, since our big chart was up to this point a mumbo-jumbo of hundreds of data fragments, we took another step. We qualitatively blended three curves into smoothed curve totals. One, the mean of various population growth projections for the U.S.A. Two, all raw materials and services demands. Three, the energy demand curve, which had exploded well beyond other projected growth demands, soaring far beyond the population growth curve.

While this unorthodox presentation at first bothered our classical statistician friends from Stanford, they were quick to acknowledge that statistical truth had not been violated. Our new chart of the 1960's sure as hell brightly illuminated the true facts of USA's future economic growth posture. This then-unique presentation clearly revealed the hyper-explosive growth demand situation well into the twenty-first century.

Once seen as a clear, fully integrated, holistic statement of "everything" bearing on proper containment of future population growth, perhaps the planning malaise infecting both government and private enterprise planning could be overcome—overcome in the light of an heretofore unacknowledged great truth.

"Hello, Malthus!"

Even though this explosive growth was beginning to evidence itself more clearly in the mid 1960's, what was happening? Economic growth planning to contain a then obvious population growth explosion was handled without other than fragmentary linear planning—a patch of growth here and a patch of growth there—yielding a hodge-podge of unsystematic growth with no action response whatsoever to the long-term whole of things... in short, business as usual.

As to our Lockheed study of the overall economic growth situation, we recommended to management that they consider an opportunity to pursue a government contract to set up properly structured information management systems. In turn, recognize one of the greatest potentials for future business—alternative energy sources. While it might take several decades to bring about use of alternative energy sources to any significant degree, all of the ecological indicators were leading toward a demand for near phase out of fossil fuel energy sources. Our study further urged management to consider the virtual gold mine of business opportunities latent in various research foundation archives—opportunities for any active business enterprise willing to synthesize mountains of useful but obscure data and reduce same to viable business enterprises.

We were still in the summing up phase of the above study in the early 1960's when, by pure coincidence, the State of California planning people found it fashionable to ask the aerospace industry if their advanced planning techniques on large systems would be applicable to the state's planning problems.

In turn, they asked for proposals covering a number of infrastructure areas. Lockheed elected to respond to the request for a proposal on the state's transportation network. Happily, I was assigned this task which was, coincidentally enough, a direct corollary to the study we were just finishing.

Our California transportation network study started with an observation that from the early 1960's, California's population growth was expected to nearly double by the end o the century. This was yet to be acknowledged by the State of California planners. They were looking only to the relatively mild characteristics of economic growth during the first half of the twentieth century. They had yet to recognize the accelerating exponential character of growth yet to come. The state's linear planning for patchwork growth was not the answer. (Indeed, the population did nearly double.)

With undeniable glaring evidence in front of our small Lockheed study group, we early on recognized that in approaching the transportation network proposal, we should note the then prevalent patchwork expansion of San Francisco as well as Los Angeles simply would not work on the long-term and only promised an inevitable massive gridlock.

Drawing on the evidence from our previous study, our approach was to propose a statewide transportation network based on development from scratch of two great new metropolitan centers. One would be located halfway between Los Angeles and San Francisco. The other halfway between SFO and Portland. Each new metropolis would have new deep water port facilities, an international airport and intra-state and inter-state highway connections through California's great central valley. These new metropolitan centers, in a manner of speaking, would serve as giant relief valves on future uncontainable patchwork growth in the greater Los Angeles area and in the greater San Francisco area. This is not to mention the ever-increasing logistics nightmare of working on the refurbishing of inner city decay from ever-widening growth perimeters.

One of the hardest points to make in our dialogues with the state's planners was the degree to which California was not only a major economic engine of the inland economy, but was becoming increasingly involved with an ever-expanding need to accommodate growing import-export demands from the Pacific Rim. This meant, of course, that California was not merely serving itself, but the inter-state and international situation as well.

The state planners dismissed those vital points by too quickly saying, "We'll simply expand the San Francisco and Los Angeles port facilities and international airports."

We were unable to make the point in the early 1960's to the effect that whatever comes in or goes out of the port facilities or airports must be moved by truck, rail or airplane. Feeble attempts to expand existing port authorities and airports without a corresponding broad based transportation infrastructure, simply would not work in the light of the magnitude of the exponential growth visible on the near horizon. All of this, coupled with concurrent patchwork growth in intra-state commerce and related infrastructure was only promising a massive gridlock in the decades to come.

Parenthetically, note that the above dialogue with the state's planners took place over thirty-five years ago. Do recall recent press releases reporting Los Angeles and San Francisco enduring the worst traffic bottlenecks and gridlocks in the entire nation. While gridlocks are bad across the nation, California's San Francisco and Los Angeles were measured as far worse by a substantial margin. The planners were asleep in the sixties. They are still asleep in this dawn of the twenty-first century.

Actually, in viewing California's planning situation, we found the best overview in the flight metaphor. With little adaptation, the OFA doctrine served quite well. In a manner of speaking, we were dealing with "three dimensions of flight" and one dimension of time. That is to say: California's very economic survival should be based on viewing desired operational conditions at the end of the century as a planned destination. Then, from the "takeoff" time toward that destination, plan for and deal with "in flight conditions" which would be encountered along the way so as to reach the planned destination "on time."

"On time" would be defined as finding that the operational situation had been properly reckoned with and was keeping pace with economic growth.

Thus, the OFA doctrine, with a "critical path network" plan, could, with little procedural modification, become a most useful tool for realistic, long-range, growth-oriented, state infrastructure planning. More of this study, including a realistic attempt to apply it to the real world, will be shared with the reader in the next chapter.

The short of it all is that after spending a very large amount of Lockheed's allotted general research budget on the two above studies, Lockheed decided that the political implications were more than they wanted to take on at that time. They withdrew from further pursuit of a state contract and related non-defense opportunities.

In any event, my life was about to take another unexpected turn.

Before President Root could put me on still another assignment, he was suddenly promoted out of the Missiles and Space Company. He was called back to corporate headquarters in southern California as Corporate Group Vice-President over other subsidiary Lockheed companies.

Root left me without a backward glance toward the impact his leaving would have on my career. This would have been understandable if he had not earlier taken it upon himself to wipe out my Boeing opportunity. This left me somewhat bitter since the man who replaced Root as president did not want me on his staff. I had previously found myself in open disagreement with him and I didn't feel he had the leadership qualities for the position, though I don't deny he was a quite intelligent man. Top corporate management, as it turned out, later came to the same conclusion and fired him from the job as president.

In any event, I was transferred back to the Missiles Division. Oh, unhappy day. The relationship with Vice-President Burriss. While still reporting to him in an "Assistant to" capacity, I was given no staff and moved to a remote hole-in-the-wall office, doing meaningless tasks such as document review studies, whatever the hell that meant. I was beginning to witness my chair slowly being pulled out from under me.

However, the fates were conspiring again, but I still wasn't listening hard enough. There was no possibility of reactivating the Boeing situation under the circumstances, and yet I knew I was going to have to take some action soon.

With an uncertain future in mind, we sold our second Los Altos home and moved into our Carmel beach house. My wife had become a very successful fine artist, showing in top galleries in Carmel and San Francisco. We had earlier purchased a three bedroom adobe cottage on the upper side of one of Carmel's waterfront roads with a spectacular view of the entire Carmel Bay. It was rather small, but we had built a detached artist's studio for her and found the home quite comfortable.

For a few months, I drove the long commute from Carmel to

Lockheed every day, while pondering just what I would do. Hope for any future role with Lockheed diminished daily. But then, too, I realized that I was very much intrigued with the non-defense studies I had done while reporting to Root. Then came "a blinding glimpse of the obvious." I was bone weary of working on weapons systems. I also had to admit to the feeling of drowning in the murky waters of corporate politics.

"Now you're listening," said the conspiring fates. I yielded to a Greater Wisdom and left big corporation life forever. After twelve and a half years with Lockheed and now at age forty-five, I had finally come to the conclusion that this maverick—particularly a maverick whose strong doctrinal convictions too often found him in conflict with the conventional wisdom—was simply not cut out to be a big corporation political animal.

In retrospect, and as a footnote to many years with big corporations—and certainly without the bitter taste I had upon initially leaving Lockheed—I would caution any professional never to allow himself to be persuaded by company loyalty. Oh, yes, indeed, one must maintain his personal integrity and ethical behavior. But do not make the mistake of depending on reciprocal corporate loyalty. With possible rare exceptions, corporate loyalty to an individual in a big corporation simply does not exist.

Moreover, to anyone aspiring to a big corporation career, I would also strongly urge they make a special effort not to flunk "Corporate Obedience School." No, this school won't be found delineated in any corporate policies and procedures manual. But believe me, having flunked Corporate Obedience School, I know it exists. It has a strong unwritten curriculum. An individual, if he is ethically motivated, can easily find himself ethically correct, but in the corporate sense, politically incorrect. There are many good people in big corporations who maintain their personal integrity by keeping their mouths shut at times, while acquiring a feeling for the corporate nuances of getting their views across in more subtle ways. These people get good grades in Corporate Obedience School. Other less ethical people simply kiss ass and also get good grades. As a maverick, I simply was not congenitally wired to play that game.

In retrospect, notwithstanding Lockheed and Boeing career machinations, I was not aware that all the while the conspiring fates were steering me away from the big corporation life and toward professional independence. I was just slow getting the message.

As a last request, I asked Lockheed if I might have the last two studies I had done while reporting to former President Root. Of no further interest to Lockheed, they released this potentially valuable material to me, though I had no idea at the time as to how I might use it.

In any event, I was out of the big corporation life forever, and, once again, new horizons lay ahead.

Chapter Seven
The Dimensions of Professional Independence
Emergence of the Odyssey's Purpose

In this last chapter, covering the remaining decades of an eighty-year odyssey, surprising and unexpected changes in my professional career led to much indirect, additional input into an ecologically premised approach to things.

When I say "ecologically premised," I am not referring only to the generally understood limited definition of that term. While even the limited definition of ecology is not yet widely heeded, the common definition of "Ecology" is: "The science of relationships between and among all life forms and their environments... and their impacts upon one another under various conditions." All of this, of course, relates to the welfare of mankind as a whole.

In the process of reacting to the above definition, the Industrialists and the Environmentalists are in a constant state of antagonism toward one another. This has led to the dangerous advocacy of *two* environments—natural and man-made. Whereas, if we can come to accept new advocacies of ecology as offered by a few unsung top scientists, together with a synthesis of their advocacies, there will then be a path to *one* spiritually and ethically premised new ecology— a path toward *one* integrated world ecosystem.

While the above preamble somewhat preempts a new ecological advocacy offered in the Epilogue, it seemed appropriate at this point, in the light of professional exposure of a different kind yet to come, to at least hint at the endpoint of my odyssey.

The first few weeks in Carmel after leaving Lockheed we spent relaxing and regrouping while enjoying the search for a beach front building site and designing a larger home and studio. We were fortunate in securing one of the remaining few ideal sites—a pie-shaped site with a one hundred eighty foot beach frontage just south of the mouth of the Carmel River.

With many years of extra-curricula studies behind me of architectural design and construction methods, designing and building was not only a joy, but good therapy. Somehow, watching a definitive end point appear in substantive form over a short period of time with no "committee" involvement other than my wife, was a great feeling. Our beautiful design offered lots of floor to ceiling plate glass in our two-story home, with an elevation on the slope above the beach such that we had an incomparable view of the entire Carmel Bay from the rugged cliffs of Point Lobos State Park to the south, then north to the town's Carmel Point and across the bay to the Pebble Beach Lodge.

Supervising a crew of hand picked craftsmen who were not only good at their respective crafts, but who took pride in their work and in their congeniality with fellow craftsmen, was a real pleasure. As is always the case with a complex, two-story, one-of-a-kind house on a hillside, many details arise during the construction process involving integration of various subsystem problems—particularly when the basic objective includes preserving the aesthetic integrity of the design. Working out these problems harmoniously, with only a few good-natured disputes from time to time, was an additional bonus. Moreover, most of our crew, though working on other projects from time to time, were with our small company for more than twenty-five years. These craftsmen also had long-term building lineage behind them. At one point, we had four father and son teams on our projects.

On each project, the icing on the cake, of course, was to behold the palpable presence of a beautiful finished product, rendered with harmony and comradery.

Then, too, actually living the waterfront experience in one of the most beautiful meetings of land and sea in the whole world offered pleasures we hadn't fully expected or imagined. Glorious sunsets, moonlight on the water, storms coming and going, wild surfs on some days, lake-like calm on others. On those quiet mornings, the only sounds were the crying of sea gulls or the sounds of clamshells cracking. The sea otters would place small rocks on their chests and with their little hands crack open the shells as they floated lazily on the gentle swells.

Our sixty-power telescope was also kept quite busy with yacht races on the bay, ships passing north and south, or an occasional ancient schooner sailing into the making of a movie.

One of our greatest thrills was to wake up just after dawn one morning and, as we sat down for coffee at the window in our living room, we looked out in shock. Two enormous whales were at rest in our very own backyard, so to speak. Just off the very narrow beach on our particular site, the water ran very deep on an underwater rock cliff. These enormous creatures remained at rest in "our backyard" for an hour or so, then dramatically flipped their great tails at us and took off... Great fun.

In those few happy months of building and just living life, I found much needed therapy. I must admit that I had left Lockheed with a very bitter taste in my mouth. If I had properly maintained my spiritual perspective through it all, I would have peacefully resigned at a much earlier date. But nonetheless, the conspiring fates never left my side and I only needed to have paid more attention to their often subtle messages. While I hadn't yet resolved just what I was going to do with my life, peace and spiritual perspective were reemerging.

To digress a bit, during the construction of our home, a distinguished couple walked through the house with considerable interest and asked if we could design and build a home for them in the Carmel Valley Golf and Country Club. We could certainly use the money and quickly said yes.

At that point, we took out a general building contractor's license and formed our first small independent company, which we named the Integrated Arts Company. While this first building project for an outside party was quite successful, and the clients remained enduring friends, I soon found out that my design and construction fee was seriously disproportionate to the demands made on my time. That is, it was time spent not only on design, building permit acquisition and construction supervision, but on an extraordinary amount of time invested in satisfying the client's wishes, while bearing in mind the integrity of the design as a whole. Preserving the integrity of the design was, for me, of equal importance to the financial considerations.

Too much time went into dealing with the client's many ideas, which as isolated ideas were often good, but which just as often triggered violations of the integrity of the design. But as far as the final outcome was concerned, it all worked out rather well. The clients were sensitive people and together we produced a beautiful home.

In any case, rather than pursue other clients for new projects, we decided we would eventually, when finances permitted, build and sell our own designs. In the meantime, I would take on occasional management consulting jobs and also continue to respond to speaking engagements that stemmed from many years of guest lectures given to outside institutions while with Lockheed. During that period, many talks had been given to the American Management Association, various University of California campuses and technical societies.

One lecture in particular—my first after leaving Lockheed— triggered a most interesting and, at the time, very promising opportunity to become involved in large scale land development. The president of the American Society of Civil Engineers had heard one of my talks to the American Management Association and asked if I would give the keynote address to the annual conference of their San Francisco section.

I patterned the address along the lines of the proposal for California's transportation network, developed for the state while with Lockheed. Recall the essence of that state proposal as described in the previous chapter. The proposal called for two great new metropolitan centers developed from scratch, if California was to contain an explosive, near doubling of population by early in the twenty-first century. At that time, this was some thirty-five or forty years away. My presentation of the essence of that same proposal to the civil engineers, which included several dramatic graphics projected on the large screen—very expensive graphics which had been developed with Lockheed research funds—was gratifyingly well received, and yielded some excellent, illustrated press coverage in the San Francisco Examiner.

One of the most positive outcomes of that particular lecture came through the Dean of Architecture and Engineering of the California State University at San Luis Obispo, George Hasslein. In response to that lecture, he invited me to visit his campus for a one-week period. His intention was to expose the architectural students to the broader implications of large-scale system analysis. That week on the university campus involved both students and faculty members and the exchange was most gratifying. I learned much on that visit.

On my last evening with George Hasslein, we had a most interesting dinner discussion at San Luis Obispo's uniquely famous Madonna Inn.

But first I must note that Dean Hasslein, who was also a Fellow of the American Institute of Architects, offered a quaint comment on the Madonna Inn. The inn was a gross, dramatically overstated design with enormous, protruding boulders stuffed into the construction throughout the complex. This was accompanied by exaggerated gingerbread trimming, much stained glass and copper. The men's room was a special treat. As one stood at a long urinal trough, facing a large dramatic wall of those outsized boulders, just at the very moment the magic eye struck the appropriate part of one's anatomy, a gorgeous waterfall poured over the rocks and into the trough. Indeed, awe inspiring relief. I loved Architect Hasslein's general comment on the Madonna Inn: He said, "It's so bad, it's good."

Well, back to our dinner discussion. George asked what I thought about making a presentation to the San Luis Obispo city fathers and citizens. He suggested the same presentation that was given to the American Institute of Civil Engineers conference. He further offered that my proposal for two great new metropolitan centers for California, one of which would find their city a suburb of the new metropolis, would be such that it would be interesting to hear the local reaction to such a plan. Hasslein, personally, was very much interested in such a plan. He called me at home a week later and set the date for the talk a month hence in the university auditorium. My lessons in local, county and state politics regarding land development were soon to begin.

But these lessons were first to begin on my home ground, the Monterey Peninsula in Monterey, County. My neighbor at the time, Doug Tellwright, retired Executive Vice President of Bell Telephone, had become quite intrigued with my development planning philosophy through many informal "over-the-back-fence" dialogues. He felt I should meet Tom Hudson, then chairman of the Monterey County Board of Supervisors. Tellwright arranged a luncheon at Pebble Beach Lodge. Hudson was into not only county supervisory matters, but was himself very mush into some very large land development schemes on the Monterey Peninsula.

We hit it off right away, since Tom was also a pilot. I was also quite intrigued with his airplane. In addition to his single engine airplane, he had purchased a World War II twin-engine bomber which had been converted to an executive transport. I was looking forward to flying it, since Tom was not yet rated for multi-engine airplanes. Like myself, he was a dedicated flying enthusiast and we were destined to make many business trips in his converted bomber.

Tom was also a Monterey attorney and had many connections in both political and land development circles. Since we shared a philosophy of blending land development with sound environmental practices, I soon took an office in his Monterey suite of offices. In addition to pursuing Monterey County land development opportunities, Hudson became very interested in the new metropolitan city idea in the San Luis area. He accompanied me on meetings there, which followed my presentation to the city fathers. These trips, of course, were made via my flying his bomber while at the same time training him for his multi-engine rating.

As it turned out, while certainly not everyone was in favor of the new metropolis, a sufficient number of prominent people, including the mayor and a major real estate firm, expressed considerable interest. In a separate meeting of myself, Hudson, Hasslein and the real estate firm who called for that meeting, we answered a few questions on the origin of the Metropolis Alpha proposal, and then listened to the real estate people.

They indicated they had access to exclusive representation of a seventeen-thousand-acre ranch just north of San Luis. This huge ranch, ideal as a core property for the new metropolis, had an easy, few miles access to San Luis' new deep water port and was also adjacent to existing main line railway service. Moreover, the real estate people offered that an appropriate proposal to the owner of the ranch could net us an exclusive option on the property without the constraint of having to lay out any cash until the massive project was actually ready to begin.

At this point, Hudson brought forward representatives of several land development and architectural firms he knew in San Francisco and Los Angeles. In speculative agreement, three different firms were willing to supply us with a few individuals who would work gratis through the proposal phase and until venture capital investors were secured.

The initial part of the proposal effort was aimed at the owner of the property and did not involve opening up the Pandora's Box of massive land development politics. It all proceeded smoothly and we obtained our exclusive option with landowner William Reis. Since his ranch was open land surrounded by other large ranches, we also explored the possibility of future options on huge tracts of ranch land adjacent to his seventeen-thousand acres, but also taking care not to box ourselves into future commitments prematurely.

The next and quite difficult phase was to seek a consortium of investors who were prepared to commit hundreds of millions of dollars to initial infrastructure, with an acknowledged unavoidable waiting period for a return on their investment. That is, until cash sales were made to individual land developers who would buy carefully delineated purpose-oriented parcels of the new city plan. Land developers would also be required to endorse ecologically balanced delineations of commercial and residential areas with careful regard for the ecotone between the new city and the adjacent national forest. But first, we had to advise the state of California planners of our intent, since they would eventually be heavily involved in the approval process.

Through Hudson's connections, we opened up discussions with the state's planners. Some of the planners were those I talked to while working on the Lockheed proposal. At that time, the State of California had not reacted to the proposal efforts of other aerospace firms on various transportation, energy, water and other infrastructure planning problems; that is, other than to modify some of their information management systems. Otherwise, it was business as usual. The state's initial reaction to our proposal was somewhat indifferent, as it was during our Lockheed proposal effort, but not totally discouraging. Some of the planners thought we would be deep into political difficulties if we talked about too large a program too soon.

Perhaps we should have cooled off somewhat in light of the state planners' indifference, but they had not actually said, "No." In fact, some of the planners were in favor of the idea, but they were locked into "group think." So, we proceeded on with our small consortium and developed an initial basic plan. The plan was only intended to be of sufficient scope to start approaching potential investors.

Sadly, a couple of hard years of intense effort had not yielded a single investor who did not fear the political ramifications of bringing so ambitious a program to a reasonably early point of return on investment. This investor attitude was difficult to reckon with, since we had to answer honestly their questions on obtaining state approval. Moreover, all of the potential investors admitted they were involved in patchwork development schemes appended to existing metropolitan centers, which of course promised an early return on investment. While potential investors understood what we were trying to do, or thought they did, their sympathies were not convertible to investment dollars. Three years effort was enough for me.

At this point, I had seriously invaded our family resources in my own end of the effort, and I would have to make some changes soon. Even my good friend at the university, Dean George Hasslein, though he still firmly believed in the program, had started calling me "The Man From La Mancha." But I had ceased finding this tag funny. I was growing weary of playing "Don Quixote." Too many windmills to tilt. My lance was wearing out.

In any event, the whole matter was very suddenly taken out of our hands. William Reis, owner of the seventeen thousand acres—the land that formed the very core of our new city proposal—had fallen seriously ill and died of cancer. He had covered this contingency legally and there was no commitment to honor our option in the event of his death. His heirs were not the least bit interested in our proposal for a great new metropolitan city.

While I had added greatly to my architectural and land development knowledge in working directly with experts from top architectural and land development firms, clearly this was not enough. I was approaching another impasse.

Flying back to Monterey in Tom's bomber, after our final and somber meeting in Los Angeles with our small consortium, I reflected on our quiet parting in which we all hoped to work together another day. Settling into the cruise mode for the clear weather night flight, Tom had elected a snooze and I found myself taking an overview of the nature of the obstacles we had encountered in presenting the proposal for great new metropolitan cities for the State of California.

In retrospect on all of this, I had to finally acknowledge—as I put away my Don Quixote lance—that the State of California's monstrous, bureaucratic political machine could not be swayed. Notwithstanding unequivocal statistical evidence of California's explosive economic growth situation, and the specter of noncontainability of that growth.

I also had to acknowledge a hard and very disturbing fact concerning land development investors. Their short-term profit thinking, in their own minds, had to be based on relatively short-term, patchwork land development, while wearing blinders to long-term consequences. They remained blind to the fact that such development practices would only lead to unwieldy appendages to existing overburdened, big city infrastructures. Unmanageable urban sprawl was on its way!

Further, in my overview, the education system at large was not to be let off the hook. They are most certainly to be held accountable for an almost total disregard of the curricular needs of the young people who would be running things in a few decades or less. The basic failure of the education system thus far lies in an overwhelming training of specialists. That is to say: Where are the generalists—the interdisciplinarians who must integrate the work of specialists and make our increasingly complex infrastructure systems perform efficiently? Education gets a "D" here.

In summary of my retrospective thoughts at this point: Bureaucrats, Investors and Educators generally understood in their heads, not their hearts, the new development doctrine we were advocating; but were so locked into the politics of the conventional wisdom, and the limitations of "group think," that it seemed they simply could not bring these new realities *into their hearts*—and, in turn, develop a new passion for reality! Yes, I know, I've succumbed to idealism.

Actually, when the new realities will take their place in the real world is hard to say. But, in the final analysis, I've come to believe that only Federal and State mandated new metropolitan cities, with big government loans behind them, will save California from inevitable deterioration in the twenty-first century. Moreover, the leaders in Government, Investment and Education must be deeply committed, *in their hearts*, to the moral and ethical implications of it all... Well, end of reflective thoughts for now. We're almost home.

"This is N739 calling Monterey Tower. We are ten miles east at

four thousand feet, requesting a straight-in approach to Runway 28...
over."

"N739, this is Monterey Tower. You are cleared for a straight-in
approach to Runway 28. Wind is west at ten. No other traffic at this
time."

"Thanks, Tower.".... Home again.

At about the same time we abandoned the San Luis Obispo
program, it appeared my speculative, non-paying work on Tom
Hudson's land development projects was going long-term with no
immediate or near future financial return to me.

Indeed, even Tom Hudson, with his political smarts, did not see
the political ramifications of bringing to fruition an enormous
residential land development project on the massive San Carlos Ranch
jus south of the Carmel Valley. As it turned out, after we had hosted
a number of potential land development firms, they, too, gave up on
persuading the local bureaucracy for approval. Nor was Hudson, as
former chairman of the Monterey County Board of Supervisors, able
to swing general opinion toward a development go-ahead.

I'm glad I didn't wait. Unbelievably, it was some *thirty years*
later that a persistent developer finally obtained a limited go-ahead
on his development proposal. But even then, in return for his permit
to proceed, he had to dedicate thousands of acres of his San Carlos
Ranch to permanent open space.

A similar pattern followed our intense effort to develop the Odello
Ranch. We presented our preliminary plan for a residential
development around a golf course, club and small hotel. After a futile
year or so of not even coming near an approval, we gave up on that
one. Another innocent land developer, unknown to us, came in and
spent a small fortune on a plan very similar to ours, with one exception
in their approach. They spent a large amount of money on an elaborate
and quite appealing scale model with beautiful architectural
renderings and many presentations to both the Carmel Planning
Commission and the County Board of Supervisors. They finally gave
up in disgust and swallowed their losses. The owners of the ranch,

the Odello family, a most gracious family who suffered through so much over the thirty years of futile effort invested in trying to add further beauty to the area, finally gave up and sold the major portion of their ranch to the state as a land preserve along the Carmel River... Well, so much for land development schemes... for now.

Though many lessons were learned through those few years of intense exposure to large land development practices, those lessons not only did not pay my bills, but my sporadic management consulting jobs were not helping much either. Even worse, I had made far too deep an invasion of our personal finances, having tilted too many windmills in apparently premature pursuit of an ecologically premised dream of great new metropolitan centers for California.

Moreover, my hard working wife, though God bless Rosemary for her support of my efforts, was carrying far too much of the financial burden... Reluctantly, I bid a friendly farewell to Tom Hudson and moved out of his office suite and back into my home office.

A now, even more radical change in my professional life, and quite a change for Rosemary as well, was soon to take place. At this point in Rosemary's fine arts career, she had been showing quite successfully in top galleries in Carmel, San Francisco and others for some eight years.

As we sat down, eyeball to eyeball, to consider what we ought to do with my professional life and her further advancement, Rosemary posed a most intriguing question:

"Why don't you apply some of your management system theories to our personal situation and examine the idea of opening our own gallery?"

Stunned for only a moment, I said, "I wonder if some basic big corporation macro-management system thinking would work in micro—in a small corporation?" I answered my own question. "Yes, Love, off hand I think it just might work very well. Let me have a couple of days thinking on it and we'll quite probably go searching for a location."

After roughing out a business plan and some basic operating requirements, we set out to search for a location. Now, finding an affordable and appropriate retail outlet location in Carmel is no easy matter. To understand this, those who are not familiar with Carmel-by-the-Sea—properly touted as one of the most beautiful meetings of land and sea in the whole world—might note that in a well run retail business, with its access to national and international trade, is a virtual gold mine. As a well-established travel agent said to me one day, "If anyone, anywhere in the world is a traveler, he will eventually visit Carmel-by-the-Sea." We soon came to find the truth in this.

In the course of working out a preliminary business plan, I realized we would have to sell our wonderful waterfront home and move into a smaller home away from the beach to raise the initial funding. We could have approached the Small Business Administration for support, I suppose, but I wanted no bureaucratic complexities in the operation. Besides, we wanted to do it on our own. Fortunately, we were able to sell our home for double what it cost us. We now had our business start-up money, along with a down payment on a very nice, smaller home in Pebble Beach.

We found an available space in a badly rundown building in a potentially excellent location—a four-unit corner building on Sixth Avenue at the intersection between the Memorial Library and the world famous Pine Inn, directly across the street. The end unit away from the corner was for sub-lease to the master leaseholder of the building. It was offered "as is" with no financial support from the owner of the building for refurbishing expenses. This particular unit was the former office of a retired doctor, with small examination rooms and a laboratory. It would have to be gutted from one end to another and be reconfigured as an art gallery—at our expense, of course. After buying any kind of lease in Carmel, one only had a ticket to rebuild the facility to his own specification at his own cost.

We had a sign painted, "Rosemary Miner Gallery," took out our City Business License, placed ads in local newspapers and a national art magazine. We hung Rosemary's paintings, which we recovered from other galleries, and opened our door for business.

153

Since Rosemary was already a well-established artist, the response was an immediate one. We were soon selling her work beyond her ability to maintain inventory. Obviously, we would have to take in other artists, and we quickly concluded that, on the long-term, this was a good thing.

We selected half-a-dozen artists who were painting various subjects in representational, impressionist and abstract modes. With this well-balanced mix of additional excellent artists, we moved on. The business was quite profitable, even in its first year. We started casting our eye on the business next door, a one-artist gallery very much in need of management. In our second year, we bought the sub-lease, retained the artist in our group, completely refurbished the unit to match our own, and cut through the middle of the wall to connect the two units. Business success was self-compounding. We added a few more artists and in our third year we were able to buy the sub-lease on the adjacent unit. Once again we completely refurbished and cut through the wall, combining the three units. Profits had escalated. Even in the face of costly refurbishing and taking out a modest income, there was enough left to cast our eye on the admittedly coveted fourth unit on the corner.

The tenant, who also held the master lease on the whole building, ran a second-hand clothing store that was not doing all that well. She was ready to retire anyway, but she had also gleaned a pretty good idea of what we were up to and she really socked it to us on the price we would have to pay to take over the master lease. So be it. We now had a very clear idea on where we were going with the business and even the building owner's rather exorbitant transfer fee on the master lease did not bother us too much. But it was done. Notwithstanding the fact that the corner unit was the most in need of repair and refurbishing, it also had a very large basement, which we desperately needed for office, framing shop and shipping and receiving. We now had a potentially fine building as an entity on a prominent business corner of Carmel.

We were now into our fourth year of successful business, and with thanks to our fine building crew not only for the complex and extensive remodeling of the building in record time, but for building our new home in Pebble Beach shortly thereafter.

I must make a special note, too, of our excellent and totally trustworthy CPA and Financial Advisor, Devin McGilloway. Devin has steered us through often-complex tax accounting problems and property sales as well as investment counseling. As a younger man with his own firm, he is still with us. I must also note our outstanding corporate and personal attorney, Tony Karachale, whose counsel helped keep our business legally tidy and eventually saw us through the sale of our gallery corporation. Also a younger man, he is still with us.

Agreeing, of course, that Rosemary would remain our star artist, specializing in seascapes, we would continue to bring in a wide range of artists in all categories of fine art. We also felt it was time to change the gallery name to a more generic one. We incorporated the business as "Miner's Gallery Americana Corporation." At that time we wrote a new, long-range business plan, a classical Input-Process-Output-Feedback model and a one hundred page Policies and Procedures Manual. Artist and client treatment, as well as rigorous, high-intensity staff training on gallery integrity was particularly emphasized.

A pivotal point on this matter of gallery integrity might be of interest. As we grew in the scope of our operation, we were able to bring in highest quality artists from all over America as well as from Canada, England, France, Spain, Africa, China, New Zealand and Australia. In addition to our proper presentation and promotion of the artist's work, we offered each artist our "Full Disclosure Policy," which was unique to the fine arts gallery business on consigned artwork. Full disclosure meant that every month, the artist was presented not only his check for the month, but an actual copy of his page out of our accounting journal. This showed him the status of his sales, whether cash or terms, and when a particular painting or sculpture sale would be confirmed by term pay off. We had also established a trustee account for *the artist's money*. Unlike sad practices we had too often encountered in other art galleries, we *never* "borrowed" artists' monies. Moreover, individual artists had the prerogative of drawing on the trustee account, based on the need, bookkeeping inconvenience notwithstanding... The word got around on our Gallery American policies and procedures and greatly enhanced our acquisition of additional high quality artists; finding us eventually stabilized with a roster of sixty-five outstanding artists across a full spectrum of prices, styles and subject matter.

Naturally, we encountered many problems in the process of developing Gallery Americana in such a way that we lived up to our own standards. While these problems were, for the most part, resolved harmoniously, there was one, particularly large problem—the very old and poor condition of the building. The building conversions noted earlier did not come easy and would have represented a prohibitive cost in loss of time but for Carmel's highly competent Chief Building Inspector, Fred Cunningham. We spoke the same language and he was not the least bit intimidated either by Carmel's cumbersome change-approval process, or by the interpretive good judgement required to blend old building codes with new building codes, tying in with city infrastructures... and getting on with it. Thanks to his fine support, we turned out a beautiful, architecturally integrated, better-than-new building on an important corner of the City of Carmel-by-the-Sea.

As the business grew, we eventually acquired the master lease on the three-level building next door. It was in worse shape than the corner building. Again, thanks to Cunningham's support, we tore it down to a shell and reconfigured it to our needs, attaching the two buildings through a center passageway.

We now had one of the larger commercial fine arts galleries on the West Coast. With the required space, staffing and posture we were able to become a significant participant in the national and international art marketing scene.

It should be noted that I have barely scratched the surface on the background issues and details involved in growing Gallery Americana to its stature at that time. One day I may write a separate book on the whole fine arts business world and the experiences involved in identifying with that world in a more meaningful way. Instead, I will shortly share with the reader the manner in which the wide variety of gallery experiences tied in with my ecological management system doctrine.

It is now 1980, some ten years since founding Gallery Americana, the gallery having offered us accomplishment and reward beyond our expectations. As I sat in our upper level gallery office on a hill overlooking rooftops to the sea, I contemplated our recently updated demographic sales map of the world, mounted on one wall of the office.

Each sale had been posted with a small red dot. Naturally, there were large overlapping clusters of red dots in the San Francisco and Los Angeles areas and smaller clusters of sales throughout California. But California sales had now been superseded by the much larger share of our total business scattered all over the United States and the world. We had sales in all major countries and many smaller countries as well, such as Egypt and, of all places, the far northern country of Finland. I was very much surprised by the heavy concentration of fine art sales to Finland. Yes, that travel agent's earlier comment to me was right on:

"Any one in the world who travels will eventually visit Carmel-by-the-Sea." And we did our promotional best to see that after they reached Carmel, they found their way to Gallery Americana. We now had a mailing list for thousands of our periodic brochures, mailed monthly to our gallery patrons all over the world.

But, it is the demographic summation of world-wide sales that leads into the whole previously unseen reason for my involvement in a business completely foreign to my former background and career desires. I no longer questioned why I had taken such a step and then carried it to its present extent. As usual, the conspiring fates were right once again. The reason turned out to be just this: I now had access to the richest possible mix of professional people from all over the US and the world with whom to share ideas and philosophies as they relate to the real world in which we live.

For me, the endless round of social involvement that is a part of the fine arts business was not always invested in small talk. In addition to monthly champagne receptions in the gallery for our artist shows, involving hundreds of people, there were lunches and dinners with individual clients in fine restaurants and in our home. Many became good friends and shared informal exchanges about life in the real world rarely found in the news media.

Moreover, people visiting us were on holiday and on their best and unguarded behavior. The many corporate CEOs an executives who purchased art from Gallery Americana were not wearing their board room demeanors. They were having fun. Just to mention one rather typical incident: Not knowing who this new client was, since the initial conversation was informal without introductions, he sat down in his blue jeans and sneakers and asked what we might have in the way of large oil paintings with industrial themes. He wanted them for the foyer of his office. Yes, we might well have what he was looking for. Only as we sat down to write up his purchase did it turn out he was CEO of a major steel corporation. He was a particularly gracious, unassuming sort of person. Lunching with him later at the Pebble Beach Lodge, I gathered many valuable, further insights and confirmation of my own thinking about the steel industry as it impacted on my ecologically oriented systems design thinking... which, by the way, I had not ceased studying all the while we were involved in the gallery business and various building projects.

Indeed, the informal dialogues with US and worldwide visitors from virtually all professions were incredibly revealing. Of course, not all gallery patrons wanted to share their thoughts. And I never pushed. But given an opening, those who had something to say about an observation offered pro or con were quite willing to really "get into it."

In a manner of speaking, I was revisiting my around-the-world odyssey quite frequently. I was getting remarkable updating on a personal level even from those corners of the world I had not previously visited. Moreover, most of these dialogues with many different professions from many places, as I previously noted, added unique insights not often found in the news media. Needless to say, the weekly entries to my research journal were many.

Perhaps one of the most vital outcomes of such world-wide exposure to the professions was a sort of "professional profile" of the stereotype executives of (1) industry and commerce, (2) ecology and environment and (3) education at large. My own previous exposure had brought these profiles forward to some extent, but not to the full degree now seen.

Fundamentally, each of the three categories of executives, being understandably quite intelligent, could empathize with the respective roles of one another, but only in a cerebral sense. That is to say, they understand *in their heads*, all three roles to varying degrees. But they are seriously introverted as to what is generally felt *in their hearts*. On occasion, bringing all three executive stereotypes together in a social situation, yielded a most disturbing observation—and perhaps reveals the very crux of why we are living in a seriously eroding world ecosystem.

These executives do not resonate with one another!

An orchestration of the three executive types—an orchestration, which would, eventually, lead us away from ecological collapse, has not yet emerged. But there is, I firmly believe, an ecosystem platform which, once initiated by the education system at large, could move us in the right direction. More will be offered later on a possible path toward overcoming a *greater terrorism*—the insidious, persistent deterioration of our global ecosystem.

It is now 1990. The years have flown by with gallery clientele not only greatly expanded, but with a whole new generation of younger clients. Even the children of some of our original gallery patrons of twenty years ago were now clients of Gallery Americana.

With my Don Quixote lance still in the shop for repairs, I had ceased venturing outside the province of Carmel, except for giving an occasional guest lecture at the State University in neighboring San Jose. I did want to keep my eye on what was happening in education circles, particularly with reference toward progress being made in placing more dominant emphasis on interdisciplinary training. Sadly enough, virtually no progress to speak of. The schools were still cranking out specialists with little attention to the urgent need for a balance of generalists—a balance of generalists who would have the interdisciplinary scope to assemble the efforts of specialists into cohesive and efficiently integrated infrastructure systems. Yes, we have infrastructure systems, but they all exhibit an appalling lack of operational and ecological acceptability... and, certainly, cannot contain the explosive economic growth yet to come... More later.

During this fast moving decade of our lives, previously noted dialogues with professional clients on virtually all subjects bearing on an explosive economic growth—and, as generally acknowledged, the need for developing unique, new methods for dealing effectively with that growth—continued with many valuable perspectives which were included in my research journals. I will share a summary synthesis of these views, together with my own research, in the last part of this chapter and in the epilogue.

During this happily hectic period, we also decided on a change in climate to the sun-drenched Carmel Valley. We sold our enjoyable but often foggy Pebble Beach home and designed a rambling ranch type home on a beautiful three-acre knoll overlooking the Carmel River valley and the mountains beyond. Also during this period, our small construction company took on several residential modification and refurbishing projects. This included a condo in Carmel, which we defined as a corporate retreat for the use of visiting artists, selected clients and ourselves when we needed to stay late in town.

But even with the condo in town, we would all too often think we were free for the day, leaving the gallery in the hands of our large staff, and drive out to our valley home only to find that some special out-of-town client had called and simply had to see either Rosemary or myself. While most clients were happy to deal with their respective salesperson, the multiple buyers of the big-ticket items felt they wanted to deal directly only with the owners of the gallery. And this was alright, of course, it was simply the nature of the fine arts business.

So, after half a dozen good years in the Carmel Valley, we decided to move into Carmel. Disappointingly, all of the good building sites of desirable size had been used up. We than started searching for an acceptable existing home in need of refurbishing. We really lucked out. We found a badly rundown home on a whole acre overlooking the pine and oak forest of Carmel's Mission Trails Park, offering a pleasant ten-minute stroll through the park to town.

While the property was an unbelievable mess for a home with such potential, it was entirely worthy of rebuilding and refurbishing. The original excellent design, with a detached guesthouse, was rendered by Carmel's acknowledged leading architect at the time. We had only to honor his original design.

While the project was a money pit and took longer to finally finish house and grounds than to build from scratch, it was well worth the effort. It was even more convenient for entertaining selected clients in our home. However, we were soon looking back over twenty years of rather intense effort in founding the gallery and growing it to a solid national and international clientele. It was time to think about, no, not retiring. Heaven forbid. But we were now ready to spend more time smelling the roses and doing some other things. We decide to sell Miner's Gallery Americana Corporation and to close down our little Integrated Arts Company. Most of our wonderful building crew were on the threshold of retirement anyway.

The gallery selling process alone, even with the very competent support of our gallery sales broker, was fraught with endless presentations and ponderous levels of detail, involving all of our internal records, our attorney and our accounting firm. Though we were only a small corporation, it seemed as if the selling process was as complicated as if we were a large one.

In any case, finding the right buyer for the gallery at an acceptable price took longer than we anticipated. We finally closed escrow on the sale in December 1992. While Rosemary would, of course, continue her painting, she did not wish to be any longer identified with Gallery Americana. She placed her work in another gallery with reasoning which made sense to both of us. She did not want to experience the confusion that might arise among our previous clients in their thinking she was somehow identified with the new management of the gallery.

For the founders of Gallery Americana, looking back over twenty-three years of rich experiences, we viewed with some nostalgia the end of an era... but this around-the-world-in-eighty-years odyssey was not finished. It simply took on still another perspective.

In our newfound freedom, I must say we found the change of pace most refreshing. With financial pressures forever behind us, Rosemary was enjoying her painting on a much-reduced scale of effort, and I would now have time to wind up this odyssey of discovery with that book or two I had always wanted to write. However, I'm glad I did not start a book until after the unique exposure through the gallery to a wide spectrum of professionals from all over the world. My research journals were bulging with perspectives that better enabled me to develop many years of highly diversified experience into some kind of cohesive matrix.

Where to begin? Perhaps with my abiding interest in reconciling religion—or, more preferably, reconciling matters of the spiritual life—with science and technology. Over the years, though almost a lifetime Protestant, I was finding many useful perspectives of the truly spiritual aspects of life under One God in not only the Protestant churches, but in Catholic and Jewish faiths as well. Not to mention the writings of other less prominent faiths seeking to identify under One God, Creator of all.

In the light of this, I had earlier found it appropriate to resign from our Protestant church. One of their rather introverted tenets was to prohibit members of the church from reading any spiritual literature not authorized by the church. For myself, not acceptable! I had become quite eclectic in my religious perspective, studying tracts of truth wherever I found them.

Now, having stated my position on religion, I found it more appropriate to my thesis to seek out a spiritually premised common denominator. That is to say, a platform for discussion which would not compromise God's Truth, but at the same time would offer the professions in general—and science and technology in particular—a clear, unambiguous derivative of spiritual truth.

The broader term I was seeking in response to that thought came from the writings of noted philosopher, Alfred North Whitehead. He ever so succinctly stated: "Religion is World Loyalty!" He said a great deal more under that heading, of course, but I had the bottom line I was seeking.

I further elected another derivative of spiritual principle that had previously served my purpose without having to fight off too many professionals. That term is "Intuition," something everyone possesses, and is a spiritually premised tool for the mind. But intuition is yet to be widely acknowledged in terms of its true worth. The subject of intuition had been far more than a study of mine for many years. Moreover, I couldn't begin to count the times I've drawn on intuition to fill in the blanks, so to speak. Indeed, on more than one occasion, intuition has saved my life.

Of the many writings on intuition I've studied, one of the best is Ellie Nadel's book, "Sixth Sense." Her scientifically confirmed research on whole brain functions, with emphasis on intuition, is well worth anyone's time.

Now, having all too briefly summarized my position on religion and things spiritual, I proceeded to ask myself what central theme I would pursue in writing a book. The decade of the 1990s was at last making obvious to the world's population that our ecosystems were rapidly and critically diminishing in life-sustaining quality. While the early signs of a diminished ecology were present decades earlier, most legislators and industrialists remained quite passive in their response. Even in the face of glaringly mounting evidence, corrective actions in the 1990's were far too feeble.

As a reaction to all of that, dedicated environmentalists went somewhat bonkers. They have vigorously sought, and are still seeking, an ecological overkill. They often seek to stop various necessary development programs incident to sustaining an ever-explosive growing population, placing unbalanced emphasis on resource use restrictions, endangered species, etc., etc.

What was happening here? As I previously touched on, it was an ongoing, sometimes fierce antagonism between the industrialists and the environmentalists. Two environments were being advocated—the *natural* environment and the *man-made* environment. And all of this with the educators fast asleep. There did not exist an educational platform designed to reconcile the two environments.

In light of all this, I now had the central thrust for my book—a strong advocacy for reconciling *two* environments to *one* environment! This would mean *one* man-engendered global ecosystem, accommodating economic growth, but with some structured ground rules on how the industrialists and the environmentalists would relate to one another.

The next step was to outline an approach to the book that would lead to a destination—to a goal for mankind. This would mean a program offering a teachable omni-matrix, embracing, in proper hierarchical order, all of the elements relating to economic growth analysis.

This yielded the title for the book. I named it "The OMEGA Matrix"—the acronym offering a meaningful symbol for Omni Matrix, Economic Growth Analysis. "Omni", of course meaning "everything", Matrix meaning "that from which something is formed." But the term "Economic Growth Analysis," does *not* refer to the classical definition of economic growth analysis, but rather to economic growth as it is generally perceived—growth of population, together with resources and services demands to sustain that growth.

Then, the subtitle based on offering a platform for movement toward a definitive ecological goal: "Putting Ecological Rudder to Global Enterprise." Hence: "The OMEGA Matrix—Putting Ecological Rudder to Global Enterprise."

Well, the years flew by in a number of unsuccessful thrusts of overly ponderous and voluminous writing in attempts to justify that title. After receiving my fair share of publisher rejection slips, one editor was kind enough to suggest I was trying too hard to jam a dozen books between two covers. More focus was needed.

I took this to heart. Retaining my original book title, I decided to structure a book which, with a few carefully delineated graphics, would be held to fewer than two hundred pages. After all, my intent was to offer all professionals, particularly the educators, a guiding prospectus of sorts—an analytical hypothesis that could be fleshed out against a highly definitive, basic OMEGA structure. In short, I would focus on a rationale for the matrix. This would be accompanied by delineation of those highest order, key factors which, when measured and analyzed by OMEGA, dictate whether or not an ecological effort is moving in the right direction.

This sounds fundamental enough, yes. But the uniqueness of OMEGA is that "everything" concerning the health of the global ecosystem has been structured into a single, three-dimensional matrix in terms of the professional analyst's classical "Input-Process-Output-Feedback" model. While full operational implementation of OMEGA would no doubt require many years, educators please note: The *teachability* of OMEGA as *the way* of approaching both localized and global ecosystem problems is *immediate*. Teaching this new way of thinking could start now!

OMEGA could serve as the primary education platform for training desperately needed interdisciplinary generalists. Training them to make their highest order professional responses to the key point discussed earlier—the fact that Industrialists, Environmentalists and Educators *do not resonate* with one another! Overcoming this dilemma is the first requisite to reconciling *two* environments into *one* environment.

In light of all that has transpired during this odyssey, it is appropriate to note that OMEGA is a direct outgrowth of the earlier discussed metaphor of flight. We are, indeed, seeking to manage the "flight" of Planet Earth through three dimensions of space and one dimension of time. We must establish a planned "destination" for Planet Earth in this new century, navigating from one carefully planned checkpoint to another with the objective of reaching a destination of ecological equilibrium "on time."

More of OMEGA—Omni Matrix, Economic Growth Analysis—will be shared in the Epilogue, also bringing in the views of selected top scientists who are pressing for greater emphasis on relationships between the physical sciences and the spiritual sciences. The fuller dimensions of consciousness as they pertain to practical applications are being researched by top scientists with very promising discoveries. All of this can be aimed not only toward a new kind of ecology, but toward reckoning with *"the greater terrorism"*—the global ecosystem's diminishing capacity for sustaining human life.

So, finally, after an exhaustive condensation of "The OMEGA Matrix," and a year or so of editorial and publishing process, OMEGA was published in the year 2001… Thus, my odyssey of "Around the World in Eighty Years," for me, ends on a high note.

But by no means do I consider this the end of my efforts to reinforce my goals. As soon as OMEGA was published, I wrote this "Odyssey on wings of Discovery" or, if you will, this "odyssey of origins." I followed with still another book, "The Ecosystem Countdown."

This new book is a work in process, further advancing the OMEGA principle in an unequivocal, Law of Entropy context. The Law of Entropy is highlighted in the Epilogue, together with a few words on the heartening increase some top scientists are placing on spiritual consciousness. These scientists are now emphasizing the fuller dimensions of spiritual consciousness and ethical precepts as they ought to bear on practical applications to our unprecedented, explosive global economy.

I plan to continue enjoying dialogues with professionals of many venues to the ends of, hopefully, seeing a lifetime's work joining the works of all those who seek to serve God's Ultimate Purpose.

Epilogue
A New Kind of Ecological Advocacy

The odyssey, now at a point of contemplation of all that has transpired, it seems appropriate to share a few ideas, mine and some distinguished others, on a brief synthesis of where it all might lead— or, better, where it ought to lead.

The OMEGA Matrix, as briefly introduced in the last chapter, outlined only its general thrust. Its very broad scope suggests reading the book if one is to comprehend the matrix in all of its parameters and parts. But what can be briefly underscored here is the key factor applied to the design of OMEGA. That key factor is "Energy." The matrix, in all of its parts, is permeated by the measuring of how energy is manipulated to serve the needs of mankind. Obviously, every act of man is based on conversion of energy in some form.

Directly related to the manipulation of energy is the enormously important, little appreciated factor known as "Entropy". The Entropy Law is the second law of thermodynamics and, in essence, states that energy and matter can be changed in only one direction, that is, from usable to unusable. In the process of "usable" to "unusable", there is always some waste. Over simply, for now, that "waste" is known as "Entropy."

Now, to be sure, engineers and scientists apply the Entropy Law every day in the course of solving relatively low order problems. But its general application stops right there. The general public, as well most professionals in all fields of endeavor, offer little recognition of that term as the measure of what our errant energy conversion practices are doing to the global ecosystem.

Since the quality of the ecosystem is a direct function of *energy* converted plus *entropy*, or waste, we can readily see, at this juncture of Planet Earth's history, that entropy is out of control. We need only consider the vicious toxic cloud hanging over most of East Asia, or the price being paid everywhere over the continued use of fossil fuel energy. That, rather than placing an *appropriate level of effort* on the development of alternate sources of low-entropy energy.

As the life-sustaining capacity of the global ecosystem diminishes every year, continuing explosive population growth is accompanied by still faster rising energy-intense, high-entropy industrial growth.

Quoting Astronaut-Scientist Dr. Edgar Mitchell, who founded the Institute of Noetic Sciences, and whose credentials embrace both the extremes of operational flight and advance scientific research, he said: "The crew of Space Ship Earth is in virtual mutiny to the order of the universe."

Indeed, with excessive global entropy now heavily upon us, Planet Earth's global ecosystem is perilously close to an inability to sustain human life.

There exists a desperate need for access to some grand synthesis of the whole of things—pivoting on the *total* measure of *energy conversion* and *resulting entropy*—common to all who ought to participate in the decision-making and legislative process. While both government and education are seriously delinquent here, it is the growth-thirsty industrialists who are to be held most accountable for diminishing the life-sustaining quality of the global ecosystem. The structure of the OMEGA matrix is offered as one possible tool for addressing appropriate measures and reconciling legislative, educational and industrial actions.

But before OMEGA—or some OMEGA-like system—can gain any kind of foothold, we must bring top level recognition to a growing body of distinguished scientists who feel that physical science must be restructured to formally embrace the spiritual dimensions of consciousness as a direct influence on a new methodology for science and technology at large.

However, it is appropriate to note that the urgency of blending religious precepts with physical science is not new. The problem was very succinctly posed half a century ago by a most distinguished scientist, Dr. Robert Millikan, then chairman of the Executive Council of the prestigious California Institute of Technology. His admonition is still largely ignored even today. While Dr. Millikan had much to say on the subject, his succinct summary applies even more in this new century. Half a century ago, he said:

"Human well being and all human progress rest at the bottom upon two pillars, the collapse of either one of which will bring down the whole structure. These two pillars are the cultivation and dissemination throughout mankind of (1) The spirit of religion (2) The spirit of science."

That statement, reflective of God's Word, is a pragmatic credo which myself and others from a nonfamous level have tried, with little success, to incorporate on the firing line of applied technology. Sad to say, the two pillars of Dr. Millikan's earlier admonition are now showing severe cracks and deep fissures. These pillars are now threatening to collapse under the weight of "the greater terrorism"— the not distant inability of the global ecosystem to sustain human life.

Yes, without question, we need a basic restructuring of the fields of physical science so as to embrace the spiritual dimensions of consciousness. The excellent body of research on this subject, mostly languishing in institutional research archives, is substantial. A useful synthesis of a large bibliography on the restructuring of science is found in Michael Talbot's superb book, "The Holographic Universe."

In his chapter on "The Need for a Basic Restructuring of Science," he states, "Currently one of the best tools for exploring the unknown aspects of reality is science. And yet when it comes to explaining the psychic and spiritual dimensions of human existence, science in the main has repeatedly fallen short of the mark. Clearly, if science is to advance further in these areas, it needs to undergo a basic restructuring, but what specifically might such a restructuring entail? Obviously the first and most necessary step is to accept the evidence of spiritual and psychic phenomena."

He notes, as one example of many, that the position of the Institute for Noetic Sciences is one wherein acceptance of spiritual phenomena is crucial not only to science, but to the survival of human civilization. This assumes a face validity of spiritual phenomena throughout the ages that cannot be denied. "At least part of the reason for the lack of acceptance of spiritual phenomena," Talbot notes, "is the long standing bias Western science has had against such phenomena. It would appear that the fear of ridicule by other professionals may be as much if not more of a stumbling block as disbelief in getting the scientific establishment to treat such phenomena with the seriousness it deserves."

Talbot goes on to say: "Another feature that must be a part of the restructuring of science is a broadening of the definition of what constitutes scientific evidence. Psychic and spiritual phenomena have played a significant role in human history and have helped shape some of the most fundamental aspects of our culture. But because they are not easy to rope in and scrutinize in a laboratory setting, science has tended to ignore them."

In light of all this, together with our earlier brief discussion of the Entropy Law, it is important to note one of the more obscure definitions of "entropy" included in the unabridged dictionary: "Entropy is a doctrine of inevitable social decline and degeneration." Obviously, we must devise ways and means to overcome this entropy doctrine on a massive scale.

Correlatively, we must design ways and means to recognize a vital but obscure definition of "economy" also found in the unabridged dictionary: "Economy is the Divine Plan for humanity, the method of Divine Administration."

In all too brief summary here, "ways and means" would include (1) Aggressive recognition of the scientific and sociological research on positive applications of the law of entropy to overcome the entropy doctrine and (2) Formalizing an endorsement of "economy" on a basis of Divine Intervention in the affairs of mankind.

From this, renewed emphasis would be placed on the practice of ethics and response to moral issues in the context of a new philosophy of Governance, Education and Technology. In conclusion, may all who ought to be engaged in efforts to correct the diminishing capacity of Planet Earth's ecosystem to sustain human life, take a firm grasp on the wealth of research findings available on runaway economic growth and excessive global entropy and, in turn, subordinate the errant limited practices of today.

In short, establish a true resonance of spirit among the people of Governance, Education and Technology. Live and act with the spirit of a new kind of economic and ecosystem advocacy. Idealistic? Yes, but not out of reach. The metaphor of flight in three dimensions of space and one dimension of time, properly exploited, can be instrumental in recognizing the urgency of response to available corrective measures.

Printed in the United States
115514LV00001BA/20/A